BEHIND THE SCENES IN

PARLIAMENT

Also in this series

BEHIND THE SCENES IN AN OCEAN LINER
BEHIND THE SCENES AT LONDON AIRPORT
BEHIND THE SCENES IN A COAL MINE
BEHIND THE SCENES ON AN OILFIELD
BEHIND THE SCENES WITH A FISHING FLEET
BEHIND THE SCENES ON A NEWSPAPER
BEHIND THE SCENES IN A HOSPITAL
BEHIND THE SCENES IN AN AIRCRAFT FACTORY
BEHIND THE SCENES AT A ZOO

In preparation

BEHIND THE SCENES IN AN HOTEL
BEHIND THE SCENES IN A CAR FACTORY
BEHIND THE SCENES AT THE THEATRE
BEHIND THE SCENES AT THE GENERAL POST OFFICE
BEHIND THE SCENES IN A FILM STUDIO

General Editor: Norman Wymer

Part of the Houses of Parliament and the statue of Richard I

BEHIND THE SCENES

in
Parliament

NORMAN WYMER

WITH A COLOURED FRONTISPIECE,
26 PHOTOGRAPHS,
AND 6 LINE DRAWINGS BY
H. A. JOHNS

PHOENIX HOUSE
LONDON

CONTENTS

BOOKS BY NORMAN WYMER

BEHIND THE SCENES AT LONDON AIRPORT
BEHIND THE SCENES IN AN OCEAN LINER
BEHIND THE SCENES ON AN OILFIELD
BEHIND THE SCENES IN A HOSPITAL
BEHIND THE SCENES IN AN HOTEL (*In preparation*)
BEHIND THE SCENES AT THE GENERAL POST OFFICE
(*In preparation*)

THE TIMES GUIDE TO THE SKY AT NIGHT (Hamish Hamilton)
YEHUDI MENUHIN
HARRY FERGUSON
SOCIAL REFORMERS (Oxford)
GREAT EXPLORERS (Oxford)
GREAT INVENTORS (Oxford)
MEDICAL SCIENTISTS AND DOCTORS (Oxford)
SOLDIERS AND SAILORS (Oxford)
FROM MARCONI TO TELSTAR (Longmans)
DR BARNARDO (Longmans)
GLASS (John Baker)
ROADS (John Baker)
POTTERY (John Baker)
GILBERT AND SULLIVAN (Methuen)
ELIZABETH GARRETT ANDERSON (Muller)
WITH MACKENZIE IN CANADA (Muller)
THE YOUNG HELEN KELLER (Max Parrish)
YOUR BOOK OF TELEVISION (Faber)
etc.

ILLUSTRATIONS

PLATES

DRAWINGS

ACKNOWLEDGMENTS

IN WRITING this book, I have received valuable assistance from many quarters: from Buckingham Palace; from the Privy Council Office; from the party headquarters in London of the Conservative, Labour and Liberal Parties; from officials and voluntary workers in the constituencies; and from members of both Houses of Parliament.

I owe a special debt to Earl Attlee, who was Labour Prime Minister from 1945 to 1951, having previously served as Deputy Prime Minister under Sir Winston Churchill in the great Coalition Government of the Second World War. Lord Attlee very kindly gave me by personal interview first-hand information concerning the duties and responsibilities of a Prime Minister, the selection of ministers, the work of Her Majesty's Government and the conduct of Cabinet meetings. He subsequently read the book in manuscript form and made further important suggestions, which I adopted.

I am also greatly indebted to Mr W. H. Loveys, Conservative Member of Parliament for the Chichester Division—my own constituency—of Sussex. He supplied me with a wealth of information about the day-to-day life of Parliament, conducted me round the House of Commons, and likewise read the book in manuscript form. The book has been read in whole or in part by a number of people in different departments of parliamentary life.

In addition to gleaning information first hand, I attended sittings of both Houses to study procedure personally.

1

The Queen Opens Parliament

ESCORTED by the Sovereign's Escort of Household Cavalry, the Life Guards in scarlet and Royal Horse Guards (the Blues) in dark blue, the Queen drives in state from Buckingham Palace to the Palace of Westminster to open Parliament. Twenty minutes before the Queen left Buckingham Palace the Imperial State Crown, which she will wear during the ceremony, was taken to Westminster under cavalry escort.

The Queen rides in the Irish State Coach drawn by three pairs of grey horses. She is wearing evening dress with some of her finest jewellery. An ermine stole is draped round her shoulders, and on her head is a glittering diamond diadem, which was made for King George IV but never worn by him. Seated on the left of the Queen is the Duke of Edinburgh, in naval uniform. (If the Duke should be ill or absent abroad, the Queen may be accompanied by Princess Margaret or perhaps by some other member of the Royal Family.)

Officers of the Household Cavalry—the Sovereign's Escort— mounted on black horses, ride immediately in front of and behind the State Coach. The procession, which is headed by dispatch-riders on motor-cycles, includes a number of carriages carrying members of the Royal Family and ladies and gentlemen

11

of the Court, some of whom ride ahead of and some in the rear of the Queen's coach.

The streets along the route to Westminster are lined with troops, and extra police have been brought in to control the crowds of sightseers who have come from near and far to watch this historic pageant.

At various points along the route bands are playing. As the Queen's coach approaches, each band in turn strikes up the National Anthem, and the troops give the royal salute. Cheered by thousands of people, the procession passes along the Mall, down Whitehall, past the Cenotaph and across Parliament Square to the Palace of Westminster.

On Her Majesty's arrival at the royal entrance, under the Victoria Tower, the Royal Standard is broken from the flagstaff. The Queen is received by two Officers of State (the Lord Great Chamberlain and the Earl Marshal) who lead her up a flight of stairs to the Robing Room.

Here the Queen removes her ermine stole and diamond diadem, and puts on the crimson velvet Robe of State. This superb robe is more than eighteen feet long, and the train, lined with ermine and decorated with gold filigree-work, is over four feet wide; it is immensely heavy. The Imperial State Crown is then placed on the Queen's head. This crown, which was first worn by Queen Victoria in the year of her accession, is studded with pearls, diamonds, sapphires, emeralds and rubies. It contains over 270 pearls and more than 2,700 diamonds. One of the rubies was worn by Henry V at the Battle of Agincourt; one of the sapphires originally belonged to Edward the Confessor.

With the great weight of the crown on her head and the heavy robe hanging from her shoulders, the Queen has much to carry. To add to the burden of her attire, the ceremony itself is a strain.

The ceremony takes place in the House of Lords, the reason for this being that the Sovereign, although head of the State, is not permitted under the British Constitution to enter the House of Commons—a ban resulting from the old feuds between Crown and Parliament of Stuart times.

Attired in her robe and crown, the Queen, accompanied by the Duke of Edinburgh, is conducted to the Chamber of the House of Lords by a splendid procession comprising the four pursuivants, wearing tabards embroidered with the Royal Arms; heralds and officers of the Court in full dress; the Comptroller and Treasurer of the Royal Household, carrying white wands; the great Officers of State—the Lord Chancellor, Lord President of the Council, Lord Great Chamberlain and the Earl Marshal —wearing their respective robes of office; and, finally, two peers, one of whom holds aloft the Sword of State and the other bears the Cap of Maintenance.

The Queen walks immediately behind the two peers. She is gracefully escorted by the Duke of Edinburgh, who holds the fingers of her outstretched left hand with a delicate touch. And the heavy train of her robe is borne by pages in short scarlet coats, white breeches and stockings, and gold-buckled shoes.

Behind the Queen follow the Mistress of the Robes, Ladies-in-Waiting, and other members of the Household.

In the Chamber of the House of Lords, awaiting the Queen's arrival in hushed silence, are assembled a brilliant gathering of Royalty; peers in scarlet robes and peeresses in gorgeous dresses and tiaras; archbishops and bishops in bright red velvet; judges in wigs and gowns; members of the Diplomatic Corps in a rich assortment of uniforms with decorations; and many other distinguished people.

As the Queen enters the Chamber the dimmed lights are flashed up to full power, and the entire assembly rise to their feet; the peers in the front row bow their heads and the peeresses drop a little curtsy.

Holding her head high to balance the crown, the Queen walks

slowly and with great dignity to the dais, mounts the three steps and seats herself on the throne. The Duke of Edinburgh takes up his position by the Chair of State to the left of and one step lower than the throne; and members of the Household stand on either side of the Queen.

'My Lords, pray be seated,' Her Majesty bids the distinguished company.

The Queen then commands the Lord Great Chamberlain to dispatch Black Rod (Gentleman Usher to the Lord Chamberlain's department) to summon the Commons to the Bar of the House of Lords to hear her speech from the throne. The Lord Great Chamberlain passes on the Queen's command by raising his wand, and Black Rod, preceded by two officials from the Lords, proceeds to the House of Commons.

As Black Rod approaches the House of Commons, the Serjeant at Arms slams the door in his face to denote that the Sovereign has no access to the Commons. The Gentleman Usher knocks three times with his black rod of office. The Serjeant at Arms looks through the grille in the door, to 'identify' him, and then orders the door to be opened.

Black Rod enters, bows three times to the assembled Members of Parliament, and delivers his message from the Queen commanding their immediate attendance in the House of Lords.

The Serjeant at Arms then picks up the Mace (symbol of the Speaker's authority in the Commons) and, bearing it on his shoulder, walks slowly towards the door of the House. The Speaker, who presides over the Commons, and Black Rod follow.

'Make way for Black Rod. Make way for Mr Speaker,' shouts the principal doorkeeper.

'Hats off, Strangers,' police inspectors order spectators assembled in the corridors.

In slow procession the Speaker and Black Rod lead the

principal members of the Government and Opposition in the Commons to the House of Lords. The Prime Minister and the Leader of the Opposition walk together, and behind them, in order of precedence, other ministers and leading members of the Opposition follow in pairs.

On their arrival at the Bar of the House, the Lord Chancellor, dressed in a gold and black robe, steps forward and bows to the Queen. He then mounts the dais and, kneeling on the top step, takes the 'gracious speech' from his Purse and hands it to Her Majesty.

The Queen then reads the speech to the Lords and Commons assembled together. In this speech the Queen, as constitutional head of the State, outlines the policy and programme of the Government for the new session of Parliament now opening. 'My ministers will . . .'

The wording is framed to read as if the Queen had written the speech herself. In fact, the 'gracious speech' is always composed by the Government, whichever party may be in power, and is then submitted to the Queen for her consideration prior to the opening of Parliament. The Queen may make suggestions for minor alterations in the wording, and these may be adopted by the Cabinet, but she will never attempt to seek alterations affecting policy. To do so would be unconstitutional. Even if she personally disapproves of a policy, the Queen will read the speech as it is presented to her.

At the end of the speech, which usually takes about ten minutes to read, the Queen closes with these words: 'I pray that the blessing of Almighty God will rest upon your counsels.' She then hands back the speech to the Lord Chancellor.

The Speaker bows low to Her Majesty and leads the Commons back to their own Chamber.

The Queen leaves the House of Lords and, after de-robing, drives back in state to Buckingham Palace. The Royal Standard is hauled down and is replaced by the Union Jack, which is

15

flown every day from the Victoria Tower between the hours of 10 a.m. and sunset when Parliament is sitting.

And so a new session of Parliament begins.

When the Government has completed the programme outlined in the 'gracious speech'—which may take a year or more —the Prime Minister will ask the Queen to prorogue Parliament: that is, suspend further sittings of the Lords and Commons without dissolving Parliament. A further programme will then be formulated by the Government, and a few weeks later the Queen will open another session. She may open several new sessions during the lifetime of the Government in office.

The maximum period that a Government may remain in office, except in time of war, is five years. Before that period elapses the Prime Minister must seek a new mandate from the electorate. At a time which he considers opportune he will request the Queen to dissolve Parliament. A General Election will then be held; and, after a new Government has been formed, with perhaps a different party in power, the Queen will open the first session of a new Parliament.

2

The British Constitution

PARLIAMENT, in its modern form, is seven hundred years old, but the British Constitution has gradually evolved, through written and unwritten laws, over a considerably longer period dating back to Saxon times.

Parliament (which comes from the French word *parlement*) originated as an assembly of important men summoned by the King, who reigned almost supreme, to advise and assist him in ruling the country.

In Saxon times the King personally selected a body of men of high estate—the wealthiest and reputedly the wisest in the land—and from time to time he would summon his 'Court of Wise Men' and hold a *Witenagemot* to discuss policy, frame laws and levy taxes. These assemblies, which took place wherever the King happened to be staying, were the beginnings of the British parliamentary system.

The Norman kings, operating on a grander scale, ruled with the assistance of a Great Council—the *Curia Regis*—comprising members of the Royal Family, the Royal Household, bishops, abbots and wealthy noblemen with large estates. The Council dispensed justice, undertook various administrative duties such as collecting taxes and advised and assisted the King in all matters concerning the government of the people.

B   17

But the people had no say in how they were governed.

During the Middle Ages attempts were made to extend the Council on a broader basis by including representatives of the people instead of only favoured men of high estate. Finally, in the thirteenth century, Simon de Montfort led a revolt against this feudal system of government by the King and his Council of barons.

Simon de Montfort took the King (Henry III) prisoner, and in 1265 he summoned a Parliament which included two knights from each county and two burgesses (prominent citizens) from a number of chosen towns or boroughs to represent the people.

Thus, seven hundred years ago, Simon de Montfort laid the first foundations of modern Parliament, with its County and Borough constituencies.

The knights and burgesses made general recommendations for the government of the country and looked after the interests of their respective districts. For example, if taxation caused hardship to a section of the community, they would point out the injustices and perhaps petition the King for an alteration in the law. Sometimes they would present the King with a *billa*, showing what form the new law should take—the origin of the modern parliamentary Bill.

In course of time Parliament divided into two sections. The noblemen, bishops, abbots, judges and wealthy landowners, appointed by the King, sat in an 'Upper House'—now the House of Lords. The knights and burgesses, representing the communities, sat in a 'Lower House'—now the House of Commons. (To this day the House of Lords is known as the 'Upper Chamber' and the House of Commons as the 'Lower Chamber'.)

And so the framework of Parliament began to take shape on present-day lines.

Yet the authority of Parliament was very restricted by comparison with today. It met only at irregular, and often infrequent, intervals—normally only when summoned by the Sovereign.

Even after the establishment of an 'Upper' and 'Lower' House, the Sovereign still appointed a private Council of Ministers—called from Tudor times onwards the Privy Council —to undertake the duties of government. The Privy Councillors usually met in secret, and at these secret meetings they conducted all the business of the State now undertaken by the Cabinet. They debated policies and submitted their recommendations to the Sovereign, who then sanctioned or rejected them according to his own private judgment.

The Sovereign ruled through the Privy Council as the main instrument of government, and summoned Parliament only in times of emergency, such as when faced with the necessity of raising money for military purposes, or perhaps when he was anxious for the support of Parliament in some new measure that might arouse controversy in the country.

During Tudor times the Sovereign increasingly had occasion to seek the support of Parliament. Henry VIII turned to the House of Commons to pass the legislation required for the sweeping changes brought about by the Reformation. He could not turn to the House of Lords, since obviously the church dignitaries would have opposed him. Henry VIII rewarded the Commons for their support by granting them lands confiscated from the Church. In the reign of Elizabeth I wealthy city merchants were beginning to make their influence felt in the Commons.

For these reasons the power of Parliament increased greatly during Tudor times, with the Commons emerging as the more important of the two Houses—a complete reversal of their original standing.

As Parliament thus gained in strength, so it pressed for still greater authority. Elizabeth I was obliged to handle Parliament with great skill and tact. By so doing she managed to preserve the power of the Crown. Her successors, James I and Charles I, on the other hand, believed in the 'divine right of Kings': they held that kings were the representatives of God and that therefore their word was law. They refused to submit to the growing demands of Parliament; and this led to open conflict between King and Parliament, and became one of the major causes of the Civil War.

The struggle for supreme power continued intermittently throughout most of the seventeenth century. During this time the authority of Parliament steadily increased, while that of the Sovereign declined. Finally, in 1688, after the deposition of James II, William and Mary were compelled to sign the Bill of Rights, granting the supreme power of government to Parliament for all time.

Since then many important reforms and developments in the British Constitution have taken place, notably reforms in the electoral system, giving many more people the right to vote at parliamentary elections, and the development of the political parties. All these developments have combined to make Parliament more efficient, more truly representative of the people, and, in a word, more democratic.

Today Parliament consists of three elements: the Sovereign (*see* Chapter 3), the House of Lords (*see* Chapter 8) and the House of Commons (*see* Chapter 7).

The contest for power today is waged between the two main political parties, Conservative and Labour, whose policies for the government of the country differ greatly. Both parties have an enormous following in the country, and their struggle for power, which continues ceaselessly, is truly democratic.

The country is divided into more than six hundred constituencies, each of which elects a Member of Parliament from one of the political parties to sit in the House of Commons. At a General Election (*see* Chapter 9) the two main parties, Conservative and Labour, put up candidates to contest nearly every seat; and in many constituencies Liberals, and possibly one or two other candidates, will also stand for election. The Liberals, who never win more than a handful of seats, stand no chance of forming a government, but their elected Members may be able to influence policy from time to time, especially when the Government majority is so small that the success of a motion may depend on whether the Liberals vote with or against the Government.

The electorate vote by secret ballot, and the party which gains the greatest number of seats in the House of Commons forms Her Majesty's Government (*see* Chapter 5). The defeated party with the most seats forms Her Majesty's Opposition.

It is the duty of the Government, once elected, to put country before party and to govern in the best interests of the country as a whole. It is the duty of the Opposition, whose Leader is paid a salary, to provide constructive criticism of a kind that will help to bring this about, and to endeavour to 'bring down' the Government if it attempts to introduce measures which, in the opinion of the Opposition, are undesirable.

The Government is composed of ministers selected mainly from the House of Commons, with a few from the House of Lords. The main body of M.P.s are known as 'Private Members' (*see* Chapter 6). They look after the interests of their constituencies and play a vital role in influencing and controlling Government policy. In fact, the Government governs with the consent of Parliament.

At one time the same Parliament could sit for an unlimited period before it was finally dissolved. The longest Parliament in British history—the famous 'Long Parliament' of Cromwell's time—sat for twenty years. The shortest Parliament sat for only one day—but on that day it deposed the King, Richard II.

Today, as stated in Chapter I, the lifetime of any one Parliament is limited by Statute to five years. Thus, if the party in office loses the confidence of the people, the electorate can express their discontent and return the other major party—the Opposition party—to power at a General Election.

In practice, the party in office rarely runs the full term before seeking a fresh mandate from the electorate. Indeed, only one Government in peacetime has continued in office for the full five years—the Conservative Government of 1959 to 1964. In the normal way a Prime Minister whose party has a good workable majority in the Commons will probably decide to 'go to the country' after perhaps three or four years. But if his party has only a slender majority, making the business of government difficult or impossible, he may seek a fresh mandate from the people after only a few months, in the hope of strengthening his position.

The Palace of Westminster became the home of Parliament on account of the fact that it was the chief residence of the King from the days of Edward the Confessor until the reign of Henry VIII. William the Conqueror used to consult with his Council at the Palace as long ago as 1076. Until the sixteenth century it was customary, as already mentioned, for the Sovereign to summon Parliament to attend wherever he happened to be staying at the time. Parliament was convened at different times at a number of important towns in various parts of the country. But when the King was in London, Parliament always met at the ancient Palace of Westminster.

Originally only the Lords met in the Palace. The Commons, less privileged, had no home, and so they used to meet in Westminster Abbey, either in the Chapter House or else in the Refectory. Edward VI however considered that the Commons should also sit in the Palace, and in 1547, in the face of strong opposition from the Church, he gave them the royal Chapel of St Stephen (which stood on the site of the present St Stephen's Hall) to use as their Chamber.

For nearly three hundred years the Commons met at this spot. In 1834 most of the Palace, with the exception of Westminster Hall, was destroyed by fire, and the Palace was then rebuilt in the Gothic style with separate sections for the two Houses of Parliament. During the Second World War the Chamber of the House of Commons was irreparably damaged in an air raid—and was again rebuilt.

Today the Palace of Westminster, standing on the north bank of the River Thames, covers eight acres of ground. The front of the Palace faces Parliament Square, and running along the back of the building is the famous Terrace overlooking the river where M.P.s—as also Peers—often sit and chat together over a cup of tea or a drink.

The two Houses of Parliament each occupy approximately half of the Palace. The northern end is occupied by the Commons, and is approached by M.P.s through New Palace Yard. The southern end is occupied by the Lords, and is approached by peers through Old Palace Yard. The Royal Entrance, under the Victoria Tower, is at the south-west corner.

The two sections are linked internally by a large octagonal Central Lobby, approached through St Stephen's Entrance (the entrance for the general public) and St Stephen's Hall, the original meeting-place for the Commons. To the left of the Central Lobby, a 'Commons' Corridor' leads to the Commons' Lobby and the Chamber of the House of Commons. Beyond the Chamber are the residences of the Speaker, who presides over the Commons, and of the Serjeant at Arms. To the right of the Central Lobby, a 'Peers' Corridor' leads to the Peers' Lobby and the Chamber of the House of Lords. Beyond this Chamber are the offices of the Lord Chancellor, who presides over the Lords, and various royal apartments, including the Queen's Robing Room.

The Commons section contains numerous rooms for different purposes: a library where M.P.s can look up facts and figures

PALACE OF WESTMINSTER

SCALE IN FEET

0 20 40 60 80

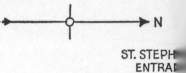

N

ST. STEPH
ENTRA

ROYAL
ENTRANCE

CHANCELLOR'S
GATE

PEERS'
ENTRANCE

STATUE OF
RICHARD I

OLD PALACE
YARD

VICTORIA
TOWER

CHANCELLOR'S
COURT

STATE
OFFICERS'
COURT

MOSES
ROOM

QUEEN'S
ROBING
ROOM

ROYAL
GALLERY

HOUSE OF
LORDS

AYE

NO

PEERS'
LOBBY

CENT
HA

ROYAL
COURT

PEERS'
COURT

PEERS'
INNER
COURT

← PEERS' LIBRARY →

MEMBERS'
DINING-ROOM

TERRACE

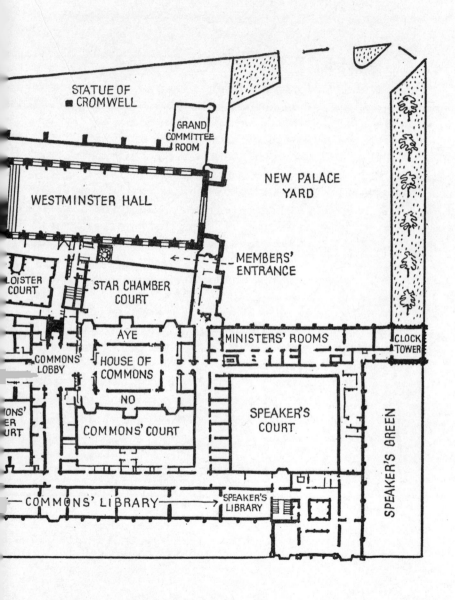

when preparing their speeches; private rooms for ministers and for chairmen of important committees; conference rooms and interviewing rooms; sixteen rooms upstairs where M.P.s do their vitally important committee work (*see* Chapter 6); offices downstairs for the 'pool' of secretaries and typists who deal with the correspondence of the Private Members; dining-rooms, and, most important, the Smoking Room where ministers and Private Members of all parties can meet inform-ally in the friendly atmosphere of a club.

The Lord's section also has a large number of rooms, some of which are used for similar purposes.

Altogether the Palace of Westminster contains some eleven hundred rooms, linked by more than two miles of corridors and stairs. The most interesting of all these rooms to the student of British political history must surely be the House of Lords Record Office, in the great Victoria Tower, which is open to the public every day from Monday to Friday inclusive. Here are housed more than $1\frac{1}{2}$ million parliamentary documents and records, including copies of every Act of Parliament since 1497.

The British parliamentary system, steeped in history and tradition, has long been the model for democratic government. Many countries, including most of the countries of the Commonwealth, have modelled their own systems of govern-ment on the British Constitution. For this reason, the Parlia-ment of the United Kingdom is often termed the 'Mother of Parliaments'.

CHAPTER

3

The Queen

UNDER the British Constitution all administrative acts of government are carried out in the Queen's name, under the style of 'Her Majesty's Government', but the responsibility of government rests with the ministers.

In theory the ministers advise the Queen on all matters of government policy, but in practice the Queen is virtually bound to accept their advice. If the Queen were to exercise her royal prerogative and reject their advice, her ministers would almost certainly resign, and this would probably lead to a General Election fought on the issue of 'Crown versus People' and this, in turn, might result in the overthrow of the monarchy.

The Queen must never indulge in party politics. The party in power—either Labour or Conservative—has been freely elected by the people and, whatever the Queen's private views may be, she must always give the Government, regardless of party, her full support. Governments rise and fall, but the Queen, as head of the State, is always in office, symbol of the country's unity. The Queen is respected by people of all parties, and therein lies her strength.

Although the Queen is bound by the advice of her ministers, she nevertheless has the right to be consulted by them on all matters. In times of crisis the ministers concerned will inform

27

and consult the Queen about every move. The Queen is entitled at all times to express her opinions on any issue about which she may have doubts. If she considers a proposed measure unwise, she may question its wisdom with the Prime Minister and warn him of the possible consequences of such a policy.

The Queen, being always in office and above party, is in a position to view every problem with complete detachment, and to form a balanced judgment of the issue in question. The Queen may be able to offer advice based on her experience of previous administrations, and this may be very valuable to a Prime Minister—especially to a Prime Minister whose party has been out of office for a long time and most of whose ministers have had little or no previous experience of government.

The Prime Minister, or indeed any minister, will always give the Queen's advice most courteous consideration. He may decide to modify his plan in accordance with the Queen's suggestions, thereby possibly avoiding a dangerous pitfall which might embarrass his Government. At the same time, the Prime Minister is at complete liberty to reject the Queen's advice; and, if he should do so, the Queen will not attempt to enforce her will.

The Queen keeps herself extremely well informed about both home and world affairs. Every evening, when Parliament is sitting, she receives a special report of the business conducted during that day and informing her of the mood of the House of Commons. She then follows this up next day by reading the official verbatim report of the proceedings in *Hansard*.

Every day she reads *The Times* and many other newspapers, including the 'popular press', and during the course of the week she also reads a great many reviews and periodicals. These newspapers and journals are first scanned by members of her staff, who mark all the items which they consider it essential or desirable for the Queen to read. In this way the Queen studies all shades of opinion concerning both world and home affairs.

But, of course, the Queen's knowledge of world affairs is not confined to reading. She is constantly meeting important people and gleaning information first hand, and her frequent tours abroad add greatly to her knowledge. There can be few people in the world as well informed as the Queen.

The Queen sees Cabinet papers and numerous Government documents. Besides this, Her Majesty receives all the Foreign Office telegrams and ambassadors' dispatches. Every day the Queen has a large number of documents and dispatches to read. They are sent to her in special dispatch cases, known as 'The Boxes', bearing the words 'The Queen' in gold letters.

Many of the reports are verbose, and deep concentration is sometimes required to grasp the meaning of certain passages. Edward VIII, during his short reign, found 'doing his Boxes' a 'relentless grind', and no doubt other Sovereigns have felt the same way. But the Queen, like her father and grandfather, attaches the greatest importance to her Boxes, and wades through the mass of documents with a critical eye, drawing attention to any suspected errors and querying any points which she may consider require clarification.

As a general rule the Queen begins to 'do her Boxes' in the morning. She returns to them at different times of the day as her many other engagements permit, and nearly every evening she finds it necessary to devote a further hour or two to reading the dispatches in order to complete this formidable and exhausting task before she goes to bed.

The Queen's programme of work naturally varies from day to day according to her public engagements. She has an early breakfast and then, her engagements permitting, retires to her study at the back of the Palace and settles down to governmental business. On her desk are photographs of her husband and children and a vase of fresh flowers.

Her private secretary brings in the first of the Government papers. Usually the Queen deals first with correspondence from her ministers, some of whom may have written to her about matters concerning their respective departments. Next the Queen deals with the numerous official documents of one kind and another which her ministers may wish her to read and approve—documents relating to various new governmental proposals. The Queen signifies her approval by writing in her own hand 'Approved—E. R.' Finally, the Queen turns her attention to her Boxes.

When the Queen is away from London she is kept constantly informed of State affairs and the most important documents are sent to her.

In addition to all her reading and correspondence, the Queen gives audiences to ministers, ambassadors, High Commissioners and others, including many persons from the Commonwealth overseas.

Once a week—usually at 6.30 on Tuesday evening—the Queen will give an audience to her Prime Minister. At this meeting, which is both informal and friendly, the Queen and her Prime Minister will discuss general affairs of State, with no other person present. This weekly audience is a regular routine, but the Queen may see her Prime Minister at other times during the week as well.

The Queen will grant an audience to her Prime Minister (or to any other minister) at any time that he may request one. And the Queen may herself summon the Prime Minister to the Palace if she should wish to consult him about some matter.

The Queen, as head of the State, works in close accord with the Prime Minister, as head of the Government. The one act in which the Queen is still constitutionally empowered to exercise her royal prerogative is in the choice of her Prime Minister.

CHAPTER

4

The Prime Minister

THE office of Prime Minister is a comparatively modern creation. It began to evolve in the eighteenth century through the inability of George I, a German, to speak English.

Prior to the reign of George I the Sovereign usually presided over Cabinet meetings. George I, having no English and being therefore unable to take part in the discussions, found this a tedious business. So, after a time, the King began to absent himself, and his chief minister Robert Walpole then conducted the Cabinet meetings in his stead.

Thus Robert Walpole became in effect Britain's first Prime Minister. He was never termed Prime Minister, however. Some time later the most senior minister in the Government came to be known as the 'Premier', and eventually, towards the end of the last century, the title of 'Prime Minister' was adopted. Yet it was still only an unofficial title. The post was finally established legally under the Ministers of the Crown Act of 1937—only about thirty years ago.

Although the Queen is constitutionally empowered to choose her Prime Minister, she will never take this upon herself if the party with the majority in the House of Commons has an established leader. After a General Election, if the party in power is victorious, the Prime Minister will remain in office without further invitation from the Queen. If his party is defeated he will tender his resignation to Her Majesty, who will then 'send for' the leader of the party which has won the greatest number of seats, and will invite him to form a Government. He will then accept the invitation and 'kiss hands'—kiss the Queen's right hand—on his appointment.

In the normal way the Prime Minister is appointed by natural right as leader of his party. But if a Prime Minister should die in office, or if he should resign through ill health or for any other reason, the Queen can exercise her royal prerogative and choose his successor. Even then her choice will not be a purely personal one. The Queen will set up inquiries through various channels to ascertain which candidate for succession to the premiership is likely to prove the most suitable, and also the most acceptable, for the post. She will probably consult a number of elder statesmen, including possibly the retiring Prime Minister, before making her choice.

The Sovereign has had the responsibility of choosing the Prime Minister on several occasions in recent times, and on one occasion the King, George V, set a precedent which has resulted in a new unwritten law being added to the Constitution.

In 1923 the Conservative Prime Minister, Bonar Law, resigned through ill health and George V had to choose between Lord Curzon, a minister with long and varied experience, and Stanley Baldwin, a minister with very little Cabinet experience. Curzon appeared to be the natural choice, but the King, after taking advice, appointed Baldwin Prime Minister. He passed over Curzon because, among other reasons, he was a peer. At that time the Labour Party (the main party in Opposition) was a young party with hardly any seats in the House of Lords, and in view of this the King did not consider it right for the Prime Minister to sit in the Upper Chamber. Following this decision, it has become an unwritten law that the Prime Minister must always sit in the Commons.

The Queen has exercised her royal prerogative twice: first in the appointment of Harold Macmillan to succeed Sir Anthony Eden (now Lord Avon) in 1957, and second in the appointment of Sir Alec Douglas-Home to succeed Macmillan in 1963. Sir Alec was a peer at the time of his appointment, but he was able to accept the premiership by renouncing his peerage (impossible in Curzon's time), standing for Parliament at a by-election and then taking his seat in the Commons—the first Prime Minister ever to transfer from the Lords to the Commons.

The Prime Minister is paid a salary of £14,000 a year, and in addition he draws £1,250 of the parliamentary salary of £3,250 paid to M.P.s, bringing the total to £15,250 a year. He has an official residence in London—Number 10 Downing Street. He also has a country house in Buckinghamshire—Chequers—where he can spend week-ends, and perhaps invite some of his colleagues for informal discussions in the peace of the countryside. He also sometimes invites to Chequers important visitors from overseas. During the Second World War Winston Churchill often retired to Chequers for a few days to work in peace and quiet; indeed, he composed many of his famous wartime speeches there.

Number 10 Downing Street is off Whitehall, the centre of most of the Government offices, and is within a few minutes' walk of the Houses of Parliament. The house next door, Number 11, is occupied by the Chancellor of the Exchequer, and Number 12 by the Government Chief Whip.

A few years ago these three houses were reconstructed at a cost of about £900,000, when a new wing and extra rooms were added to the Prime Minister's residence. Today the house is divided into two self-contained sections: the State rooms for official business, and private quarters.

The Prime Minister and his family live in a flat upstairs, containing nine bedrooms, reception rooms, a study and a kitchen equipped with all the latest modern conveniences. They furnish the flat with their own furniture, make their own catering and domestic arrangements and live in much the same way as they might do in their own home.

The State rooms are spread over the ground floor and basement. Tastefully furnished and carpeted, they consist of a series of drawing-rooms, a large dining-room for banquets, a smaller dining-room for less formal occasions, and the all-important Cabinet Room where Government policy is framed. The Cabinet Room is a long room with delicately painted panelled walls, and french windows leading out to a pleasant garden at the back of the house. A large heavy table runs down the centre of the room, with chairs for the Cabinet ministers ranged along each side and at both ends. Over the fireplace, behind the Prime Minister's chair, hangs a portrait of Robert Walpole, Britain's first Prime Minister.

During his term of office the Prime Minister is personally responsible to the Queen for the conduct of all the affairs of the nation.

On taking up his appointment he selects his ministers and forms the Government—Her Majesty's Government (*see* Chapter 5). The Prime Minister has no department of his own, but he keeps a watching brief over them all, paying special attention to foreign affairs and defence. He is in constant consultation with his ministers; gives direction when required, while avoiding interfering unnecessarily; is always at hand to give advice to any minister who may seek his counsel; and, if anything goes wrong, he must take his share of the blame as well as the minister concerned.

Besides reigning over his ministers, the Prime Minister must keep in close touch with the Sovereign, to whom he is responsible; with Parliament, through whose authority he and his ministers govern; with his party, who are his supporters; and with the nation as a whole, always remembering that it was the people—the electorate—who returned his party to power. It is the duty of the Government to govern in the best interests of the people, and if unpopular measures have to be taken the Prime Minister may be wise to send his ministers and party supporters out into the constituencies to explain the measures, or perhaps to broadcast to the nation by radio and television.

Like the Queen, the Prime Minister must keep himself well informed on a vast range of subjects concerning both home and foreign affairs. To help him in this he may engage a number of personal assistants with specialized knowledge to brief him on various matters. Harold Wilson has a team of advisers in different fields. He has also started a new departure. He periodically gives a small dinner party to a group of people in a particular line of business—industrialists, scientists, bankers, or perhaps people from the field of medicine or the arts—and over the dinner table these people tell him about the inner workings and problems of their respective trades or professions. Such information may be very useful to the Government in framing their plans for the future.

In the course of his duties the Prime Minister has to do an immense amount of reading; conduct numerous interviews; fulfil countless public engagements; travel from time to time to different parts of the world; and entertain people from many lands. The entertainment is sometimes on a grand scale. The catering arrangements for an official banquet or luncheon are undertaken for him by the Government Hospitality Service.

The Prime Minister (who is accompanied by a bodyguard wherever he goes) divides the greater part of his time between 'Number Ten', where Government policies are framed by the Cabinet, and Parliament, where those policies are then presented to the House of Commons for approval.

A stream of visitors call at 'Number Ten' to see the Prime Minister during the course of a week—ministers, M.P.s, ambassadors and foreign statesmen, leaders of both sides of industry, and people from many other walks of life. And every day messengers arrive with dispatches, reports, circulars, letters, telegrams and other forms of communication—messengers from the Queen, from the House of Commons and perhaps also from the Lords, from the embassies, and from the various Government departments congregated in Whitehall and Westminster. The Prime Minister, assisted by his team of secretaries, must deal with them all.

In Parliament, the Prime Minister should be a 'good House of Commons man'. Not only must he at all times respect most scrupulously the authority of the House, but he must also study the mood of the House, which may change from day to day, or even from hour to hour, if there is a controversial issue at stake.

The Prime Minister does not arrange the programme of work in the Commons. This is done by a senior minister, whom he appoints to act as Leader of the House (*see* Chapter 7). But the Prime Minister, with Cabinet approval, formulates Government strategy in the Commons. His active role in the House consists mainly of making important statements from time to time and of either leading or winding up important debates. But the Prime Minister does not—or should not—attend sittings only when he has a personal part to play. He visits the Chamber frequently to watch proceedings and study the mood and behaviour of Members on both sides of the House.

A good House of Commons man will also spend a fair amount of time mingling informally with Private Members in the Smoking Room, or in the dining-room or tea-room. In the friendly atmosphere of the Smoking Room, as also in the other rooms, rank is forgotten and ministers and Private Members sit and chat together on equal terms. In this way—by talking, listening and keeping his ears open—the Prime Minister is able to study and assess the current opinions of Members of all parties.

The House of Commons is the source of the Prime Minister's strength, and he must be conversant with every changing mood, prepared for any eventuality. He must keep his finger on the pulse of his own party in the House, and if at any time there are murmurings of discontent he must take immediate steps to silence or placate the dissidents. This may require a firm hand or alternatively extreme tact. He must also keep his finger on the pulse of the Opposition and endeavour to anticipate their tactics when matters of a controversial nature are to be raised in the House. In all this the Prime Minister will be assisted by the Leader of the House and the party Whips (*see* Chapter 7), who feed him with all the latest news, developments and rumours.

The Leader of the Opposition will pursue a similar course as regards his party, and endeavour to anticipate the tactics of the Government.

Of the Prime Ministers of recent years, Baldwin, Attlee and Churchill—probably the greatest figure in the whole long history of Parliament—were exceptionally good House of Commons men. They treated the House with the most profound respect, and they mixed easily with the Private Members in the Smoking Room, which they all visited frequently. Neville Chamberlain, by contrast, was an exceptionally bad House of Commons man. Although he respected the authority of the House, as all politicians must do, Chamberlain went into the Chamber, as a rule, only when his presence was essential—to make a statement, to take part in a debate, or to vote—and he very seldom visited the Smoking Room. On the comparatively few occasions when he did so he was ill at ease, cold and unapproachable.

The difficulties of a Prime Minister's job—and, of course, of the Government as a whole—are determined largely by the size of his party's majority in the House of Commons.

A Government with a large majority can introduce sweeping new legislation, perhaps of a controversial nature, without serious obstruction from the Opposition. Against that, too large a majority is apt to make a Government complacent. In time it may lose its grip, govern badly and eventually lose the confidence of the country. Also, the 'extremists' in the party may press the Government to introduce measures which are not in the best interests of the country. When their demands are refused they may stir up trouble, causing a split in the party—and this no Prime Minister can afford.

A very small majority, on the other hand, makes the whole business of government extremely difficult. It may still be possible to introduce controversial legislation, but there is always a risk that the Government may be defeated if some of its supporters should fall ill and be unable to vote at the 'division' at the end of a debate. If the defeat is on a major issue of national importance the Government will be morally obliged to resign. There is the risk, too, that the Government's slender majority may be reduced by a defeat at a by-election—as happened to the Labour Government, which was returned to power in 1964 with a majority of only 5 and within three months had this whittled down to a mere 3 through the loss of a seat at a by-election. A Government with so small a majority must be always on its mettle to survive.

What is the ideal majority? In the opinion of Lord Attlee, who in his two terms of office had majorities ranging from 186 to 6, it should not be more than 100 and not less than 20. 'A majority anywhere within this range', he says, 'will consolidate the ranks of the party from the point of view of the extremists, and at the same time will ensure a strong Opposition to keep the Government on its toes. A strong Opposition helps to promote good government.'

Every Prime Minister naturally has his own routine for dealing with the immense volume of work. Lord Attlee gives a picture of a typical day when he was Prime Minister—a day when nothing of special significance was happening:

'Get up. Have breakfast. Short walk with wife, child and dog in St James's Park. Start work at 9.30. First go through all foreign telegrams. Deal with other communications. Look through agenda for the day. If there is a Cabinet meeting, look through Cabinet agenda. See several people. May see a minister, but don't spend too long over that. Always see Foreign Secretary on Monday morning for a general review of foreign affairs —most important. Have a word with Chief Whip or Leader of the House.

'At 11 o'clock conduct Cabinet meeting. Close meeting by 12.30, if lucky. Deal with documents which have been coming in during morning. Lunch with the family.

'2.15: Go to the House and remain there until 3.30 to hear at least the beginning of a major debate. 3.30: Return to Number Ten. Perhaps see an ambassador, or deal with the appointment of a bishop. May see two or three people. Spend rest of afternoon dealing with correspondence, and perhaps making a few notes for a speech.

'7.30: Dine at the House to meet other M.P.s. If able to spare time for a tea break at House, dine at Number Ten with family. Return to the House for winding-up of debate. Take part in the division. Back to Number Ten. Try to spend a short time with family. Then deal with more papers and correspondence. Read through documents until midnight or 1 a.m. Go to bed.'

Sir Winston Churchill, who kept very long hours, frequently working well into the night, expressed the opinion that the House of Commons should not always be in session, owing to the wearing effect on both ministers and Private Members, and also because the respect in which the House is held may be lessened if it meets too frequently.

5

Her Majesty's Government

MORE than a hundred ministers normally serve in Her Majesty's Government, the number varying slightly with each administration according to the views and requirements of the Prime Minister. Probably about three-quarters of the ministers will have seats in the Commons and a quarter in the Lords.

Many of the senior ministers will be given charge of a Government department, or ministry. Each Government department is controlled by a minister. The Foreign Secretary, for example, is in charge of the Foreign Office, and the Chancellor of the Exchequer is in charge of the Treasury. The Departmental Minister supervises the running of his department, instituting ideas and plans of operation in conformity with Government policy, and is personally answerable to Parliament for all decisions made and for all actions taken. He is the administrative head—the man who makes decisions and gives instructions.

The actual work of the department is undertaken by a staff of Civil Servants, headed by a Permanent Secretary. Whereas the minister is a politician, in charge of the department only for a period and possessing no specialized knowledge of the subject, the Civil Servants are permanent officials, experts in their field, who play no part in politics. They serve the minister in charge

Escorted by the Sovereign's Escort of Household Cavalry
the Queen drives in State from Buckingham Palace to the Palace of Westminster
to open Parliament.

Members of the Queen's Bodyguard of the Yeomen of the Guard carrying out the centuries-old ceremony of searching the cellars of the Houses of Parliament before the State Opening to ensure that no modern Guy Fawkes is trying to blow them up.

The Queen's Robing Room, where Her Majesty dons the
crimson velvet Robe of State and the Imperial State Crown (see next page) is
placed on her head.

The Imperial State Crown, which is studded with diamonds (more than 2,700), pearls, rubies, emeralds and sapphires, being carried to the Houses of Parliament in Queen Alexandra's State Coach.
One of the two Maces (*right*), symbolic of the Sovereign's power, which are carried in the Queen's procession by Serjeants at Arms of the Royal Household. It is here being taken into the Palace of Westminster by a Waterman.

Gentleman Usher of the Black Rod (*left*), who summons the Commons to the House of Lords to hear the Queen's Speech from the Throne.
The Serjeant at Arms bears the Mace of the Speaker of the House of Commons.

The ceremony of opening Parliament is performed by the Queen from her throne in the House of Lords, amid a brilliant gathering of Royalty, peers and peeresses, members of the Church, the Law, the Diplomatic Corps, all in a rich assortment of robes and uniforms and decorations, and many other distinguished people.

The Speaker's Procession from the Commons to the House of Lords.
Immediately in front of the Speaker is the Serjeant at Arms bearing the Mace.

The principal members of the Government and Opposition head the slow procession
from the Commons to the House of Lords to hear the Queen's Speech.

A Tudor parliament, presided over by Henry VIII.

The Great Seal of England is
affixed to Proclamations and other
public documents of especial importance.
A new design is made for each reign.
Left, a Commonwealth Seal
showing the Cromwellian Parliament;

below, the Great Seal of
Charles I.

of their department to the best of their ability regardless of his party.

The minister works in close accord with the senior Civil Servants in his department, turning to them for technical data when this is required, and relying on their expert advice and guidance in the promotion of his plans for the department. The Civil Servants supply him with all the relevant technical information when it is necessary for the minister to submit a new plan to the Cabinet for approval. They also brief him when he has to answer questions or make a speech concerning his department in the House of Commons or, if he is a peer, in the Lords.

The Departmental Minister is assisted by a Parliamentary Secretary, or junior minister, who, besides helping with the administrative work, acts as a liaison officer between his chief and the Private Members. If an M.P. requires information about the department, or if he wishes to make a complaint, the Parliamentary Secretary will attend to him. In addition to a Parliamentary Secretary, a minister has a Parliamentary Private Secretary of non-ministerial rank—a Private Member who keeps him informed about current opinion in the House, warns him of possible trouble that may be brewing and assists in many other ways. The minister also has a Private Secretary inside the department—a Civil Servant whom he selects personally—to deal with the vast correspondence and to sort out the matters requiring the minister's personal attention.

The volume of work at a few of the ministries is so heavy that the minister in charge has a deputy, known as a Minister of State, to take some of the weight off his shoulders.

In addition to the Departmental Ministers and their assistants, the Government will also include a number of ministers without departments—'Ministers without Portfolio'. The Lord President of the Council (head of the Privy Council) and the Lord Privy Seal (Keeper of the Seal), for example, are often

Ministers without Portfolio. These ministers, having no departmental responsibilities, are able to devote all their time to general duties of government. As an instance, the Lord President of the Council might be appointed to serve as Leader of the House of Commons—a post which occupies a great deal of time (*see* page 70).

A select body of these hundred or so ministers—the first to be chosen by the Prime Minister when forming his Government —will constitute the Cabinet.

The Cabinet originated as an unofficial inner committee of the Privy Council. Charles II had a large and unwieldy Privy Council. He disliked discussing affairs of State with this 'set of fellows', so he made a practice of holding private discussions with his principal officials in his antechamber, or 'cabinet'.

Today the Cabinet is the main instrument of government, but the Privy Council still plays an important part in its machinery, advising the Queen in regard to Proclamations and Orders in Council, and also fulfilling various independent functions, discharged by committees.

The Queen approves Proclamations and Orders in Council both under powers given by Act of Parliament and under the Royal Prerogative (the term given to the Sovereign's residual powers). A Proclamation is a parchment document signed by the Queen; an impression of the Great Seal of the Realm is subsequently affixed thereto. Proclamations are required for such purposes as declaring a State of Emergency in the event of, for example, a threatened national stoppage of work on the railways; altering the coinage; fixing the dates for Bank Holidays, and so on. Orders in Council, which usually total about seven hundred a year, are signed by the Clerk of the Council and convey the approval of 'the Queen in Council' to an endless variety of matters, ranging from new colonial constitutions to the closure of burial grounds.

The advice given to Her Majesty by the Privy Council will

in some cases be purely formal, simply reflecting the wishes of the Government; in other cases it will be the outcome of the deliberations of committees. A meeting of the Privy Council is normally held by the Queen, or in her absence by Counsellors of State, every three to four weeks to deal with the accumulation of business.

Although the Privy Council still plays an important role, it is the Cabinet which formulates policy and conducts the affairs of the nation with the sanction of Parliament.

The size and composition of the Cabinet depend upon the Prime Minister. Winston Churchill's famous War Cabinet of the Second World War seldom comprised more than eight ministers—a very small number. His peacetime Cabinet was in the region of sixteen to eighteen ministers, and Lord Attlee's Cabinet was about the same size.

The smaller the number, the easier it is to reach decisions and to prosecute business efficiently and harmoniously. The ideal size for peacetime is probably about sixteen, but it is not easy to keep down to this number. Certain ministers—notably the Foreign Secretary, Chancellor of the Exchequer, Minister of Defence, the Home Secretary and the Lord Chancellor— must all unquestionably have seats in the Cabinet, and ministers in charge of other important departments will also have strong claims for inclusion. In addition the Prime Minister will almost certainly be anxious to include one or two Ministers without Portfolio. The last two Prime Ministers, Sir Alec Douglas-Home and Harold Wilson, both found it necessary to have a Cabinet of twenty-three ministers.

The qualities most desirable in a Cabinet minister are intelligence and practical common sense; vision and sound judgment; general efficiency and all-round ability; an understanding of ordinary people; a knowledge and if possible some experience of the workaday world; an ability to present a case lucidly to the Cabinet, to the House, and if necessary to the

43

nation; and the strength of character to overcome difficulties and pursue a policy to its successful conclusion in the face of possible bitter opposition and perhaps personal criticism.

In forming his Cabinet the Prime Minister will look for men who possess at least some of these qualities, but he will take other factors into consideration as well as character and ability. He must endeavour to 'balance' his Government in his selection of his ministers as a whole, including those inside and outside the Cabinet.

His party in Parliament will include men of different shades of political opinion—moderates of the 'Centre' and men with more extreme views of the 'Left Wing' and also of the 'Right Wing'. To ensure unity in the party—upon whose loyalty and support the Prime Minister depends—all these different shades of opinion must be represented in the Government, if not necessarily in the Cabinet.

Then the Prime Minister should avoid any taint of 'class distinction'. His party will include men of many different social backgrounds, from hereditary peers and middle-class intellectuals to men of very humble origin. The Prime Minister should have a fair balance of men from all types of background in his Government.

Finally, the Prime Minister must consider the age of his ministers, taking care to balance age and experience with youth. Young ministers will give vitality to the Government and help to keep it modern and up to date in its views and approach. Also, the Prime Minister must look ahead and ensure that there will always be plenty of younger ministers qualified to step into the shoes of the older ministers when the time comes for the latter to retire.

The Prime Minister endeavours to appoint the best and most suitable man for each ministerial post, taking all factors into consideration.

Selecting the Cabinet ministers is a heavy responsibility.

The success or failure of the Government will hinge largely upon the Cabinet. Some men will be obvious choices, but many of the appointments will require immense thought. The Prime Minister may have to weigh the merits and demerits of several possible candidates; and if he makes the wrong choice for some of the posts, and the ministers fail, great harm may be done.

The Prime Minister can of course replace unsuccessful ministers at any time he chooses. But he must tread warily. If he were to make sweeping changes after a short period in office —or indeed at any time—this might be construed as a confession of failure. The Cabinet as a whole would be demoralized and the country's confidence in the Government—and perhaps also confidence abroad—might well be undermined.

If, on the other hand, the Prime Minister chooses his Cabinet well and wisely, the ministers will work as a team, all pulling together with the sole aim of good government. After a short time the Cabinet will begin to develop a certain personality.

Although the Prime Minister selects his ministers, it is the Queen who actually appoints them. Technically the Cabinet is still an unofficial committee of the Privy Council, and for this reason every Cabinet minister is appointed a Privy Councillor, giving him the right to use the prefix 'The Right Honourable' before his name.

As soon as practicable after his appointment the new minister attends a meeting of the Privy Council held by the Queen and attended by three or four existing Privy Councillors, one of whom will normally be the Lord President of the Council. The new Privy Councillor kneels on his right knee on a footstool before Her Majesty and takes the Oath of Allegiance. He then moves forward, kneels on a second footstool and 'kisses hands'. He then rises and, standing, takes the Oath of a Privy Councillor, binding him to secrecy in regard to information received during his duties as a Privy Councillor. Ministers ranking as Secretaries of State (such as the Foreign Secretary and the

Home Secretary) who are to receive Seals of Office are also required to take the Oath of Office, swearing that they will well and truly serve Her Majesty in their new offices.

The Cabinet normally meets once, or possibly twice, a week. In addition there are Cabinet Committees which meet more frequently to discuss matters not requiring the attention of the full Cabinet.

Before a Cabinet meeting the various ministers work out what matters (if any) they wish to put forward for discussion. A minister must not waste the Cabinet's time by bringing up issues which he can perfectly easily decide for himself, but if he has a scheme which affects Government policy, or which may involve another ministry, he must consult the Cabinet and obtain their approval before proceeding with the scheme. This applies to all Departmental Ministers, including those not in the Cabinet. A minister outside the Cabinet must also submit his plan for approval, and he may be invited to attend the Cabinet meeting at the time when it comes up for discussion.

When the ministers have listed the subjects they wish to raise an agenda is prepared by the Cabinet Secretariat, a body of confidential clerks and secretaries, men and women, who handle all Cabinet business. Meanwhile each minister who has an item on the agenda will produce, with the assistance of Civil Servants in his department, a Cabinet Paper briefly outlining his plan and stating as concisely as possible the various arguments in favour of its adoption. These Cabinet Papers are circulated to every member of the Cabinet at least two days before the meeting, thereby giving each minister the opportunity to study in advance all matters coming up for discussion.

The Prime Minister normally conducts a Cabinet meeting. His handling of the Cabinet will probably be influenced to some extent by his personality and temperament. There was a striking contrast, for example, between the tactics of Churchill and of his opponent Attlee. Churchill, as might be expected, talked a great deal and tended to dominate the Cabinet on occasion. Attlee, on the other hand, spoke very little and conducted the meetings with quiet efficiency in the nature of a chairman of a committee.

In conducting a Cabinet meeting, the Prime Minister must control, and if necessary silence, ministers who talk too much—ministers who try, as some do, to air their views on every item on the agenda. And he must draw out the more retiring ministers who by contrast seldom open their mouths.

A minister should state his case clearly and succinctly, amplifying the details in his Cabinet Paper, and then close. There will then follow a general discussion on the pros and cons of the plan, the political implications, and how it is likely to be received by Parliament and the nation. The Prime Minister will then sum up the discussion and ask the ministers if they agree to the adoption of the plan. No vote is taken. The Prime Minister simply 'puts the question', and if the consensus of opinion appears to be in favour the plan is approved.

With a controversial issue the Cabinet may be very divided. The Prime Minister may then guide the discussion and try to find a compromise which will produce general agreement.

Once a decision is reached the entire Cabinet share the responsibility for the measure adopted. If an individual minister is strongly opposed to the measure, and is unwilling to be a party to it, the only course open to him is to resign. He is unlikely to resign, however, unless he has very strong feelings on the subject. It frequently happens that a minister is not personally in favour of a particular line of action, but in the normal way he will fall in with his colleagues, recognizing that the Cabinet must work as a team.

In attendance at the Cabinet meeting, sitting on the right of the Prime Minister, will be a member of the Cabinet Secretariat. He takes no part in the discussions. As each item on the agenda is taken he prepares a report of the proceedings—the

'Conclusions'. After the meeting a copy of the Conclusions will be sent to the Queen.

Some of the new measures approved by the Cabinet may also require the sanction of Parliament. Each minister concerned will then have to present and put forward a strong case for his plan in a debate in the House of Commons (*see* Chapter 7).

Finally, when the sanction of Parliament has been obtained, the plan will be put into operation by the Civil Servants in the department.

Like the Prime Minister, a Cabinet minister—and indeed every senior Minister of the Crown—has a very full programme of work. Ministers in key posts, such as the Foreign Secretary, Chancellor of the Exchequer and Minister of Defence, carry an especially heavy burden.

A minister in charge of a department will probably spend the morning (or the greater part of it) at the ministry attending to a hundred and one administrative matters in consultation with his Private Secretary and perhaps also his Parliamentary Secretary.

If he is a Member of the Commons he will almost certainly spend some time in the House during the afternoon and evening. He may have a statement to make, or questions to answer, if it is his day for this (*see* page 71). He may take part in a debate and then vote at the division at the end of the debate; or he may simply watch proceedings. While he is at the House he may sandwich in one or two interviews with Private Members who may wish to see him.

Then there are the Cabinet meetings to attend, and perhaps Committee meetings too (*see* page 55). From time to time he may have to travel to different parts of the country to inspect operations being undertaken by his departments. He may have to go abroad.

There are no set hours of work for the ministers of Her Majesty's Government.

CHAPTER

6

Private Members

THERE are 630 Members of Parliament, including ministers and Private Members, in the House of Commons, and they are drawn from all walks of life. There are lawyers, writers, doctors and scientists, business men, industrialists and trade union officials, farmers, railway clerks and engine drivers, miners, and people—both men and women—from many other trades and professions.

Some M.P.s are wealthy men with 'interests in the City', or with seats on the boards of large public companies. Some have no private means and are entirely dependent on their parliamentary salaries. Many come of working-class families and have had a hard struggle to reach their present position.

Thus the House of Commons represents all sections of the community, both rich and poor—a truly democratic body.

Some Private Members—notably lawyers, journalists and business men—continue to work part-time at their old professions after their election to Parliament, but this is not possible in the case of M.P.s previously employed in many of the trades and industries, such as mining, for example.

There are two schools of thought about the desirability of an M.P. having a second job outside Parliament. One school considers it advantageous (regardless of the financial aspect) because the experience broadens the M.P.'s outlook and helps him to keep abreast of the day-to-day problems of the business world—a great asset. The second school considers it undesirable for an M.P. to have a second job, on the grounds that inevitably this must interfere with his parliamentary duties.

An M.P. is now paid a good living salary of £3,250 a year and, in view of this, many people feel that he should devote all his time to his parliamentary work, the volume of which seems to increase with every year. Although this is a feasible argument, an M.P.'s salary is not as princely as it may sound, since he has very heavy expenses to meet.

An M.P. living outside the London area—as the great majority do—will require accommodation within easy reach of Westminster for four nights a week when Parliament is sitting. This, with all his meals and many incidental expenses, may cost him as much as £750 or even more a year. His correspondence will involve him in further heavy expenditure on stationery, postage and secretarial or typing fees. Another formidable item will be his travelling expenses. An M.P. is allowed free railway warrants, or alternatively a car allowance of $4\frac{1}{2}d$. a mile, for his journeys between his home and the House of Commons. But he has to pay for all his travels in his constituency—which may amount to a great mileage—out of his own pocket. These and sundry other expenses may well swallow up well over a third of an M.P.'s salary.

It is for each individual M.P. to weigh the advantages and disadvantages of taking on part-time work outside Parliament. But when an M.P. is appointed a minister he has no further choice in this matter—he must immediately relinquish certain posts he may hold, including the directorships of companies. He is also required to reveal his financial interests in companies; and, if there is a possibility of the Government doing business with any company in which he is financially interested, he may be required to sell his shares in that company. A minister must

50

devote himself entirely to his governmental duties, with no possible risk of his actions being influenced by motives of personal profit.

Many M.P.s make politics their career from the outset. On leaving school or university, a young man—or a young woman —may obtain a post in the administrative offices of one of the political parties. After gaining valuable knowledge and experience of the internal workings of his party, and of the party system generally, he will in due time try to get himself selected as a candidate for one of the parliamentary constituencies, either at a General Election or else at a by-election.

In the first instance he may have to contest a seat which his party has no hope of winning. Although faced with the certainty of defeat, he will gain excellent experience in canvassing for votes, addressing meetings, answering awkward questions, and perhaps in dealing with hecklers. On the next occasion he will probably be selected to contest a seat where his prospects will be brighter—perhaps a 'marginal' seat, where he will have the opportunity really to prove his worth. Eventually, after contesting perhaps two or three constituencies, he will achieve victory and become a Member of Parliament.

Great is his feeling of pride and excitement when the result of the contest in his constituency is announced and he addresses his constituents for the first time as their M.P. to thank them for returning him to Parliament. Inevitably he feels a certain air of importance.

He soon loses this feeling when, armed with a briefcase— which all M.P.s seem to carry—he walks into the Palace of Westminster through the Members' Entrance in New Palace Yard to take his seat in the House of Commons. At once he is bewildered by the maze of corridors and mass of enormous doors. He feels completely lost. He wanders around, exploring the geography of the place. 'Where does that door lead to?' he wonders. 'Is it the door of a minister's room? Or of the

51

library? Or . . .' Hesitantly, he opens the door a chink—and finds that the room is merely a wash-room! He puts his brief-case on a shelf in one of the many corridors—and then is unable to find it again. . . .

There is no one detailed to show him around. However, there are many policemen on duty in the Houses of Parliament, and with their assistance he soon begins to find his way about. The policemen are most helpful, and their knowledge is remarkable. They know every M.P. by name.

Every M.P., on his election to Parliament, must first take the Oath. Holding the Bible, he repeats the words: 'I swear by Almighty God that I will be faithful and bear true allegiance to Her Majesty Queen Elizabeth, her heirs and successors, according to law, so help me God.' If an M.P. has an objection to taking the Oath, he may take the Affirmation instead: 'I do solemnly, sincerely and truly declare that I will be faithful and bear true allegiance to Her Majesty Queen Elizabeth, her heirs and successors, according to law.'

The Oath is taken in the Chamber of the Commons, with the Speaker presiding. After a General Election all the Members, including those who sat in the previous Parliament, file up in turn to the Table in front of the Speaker's Chair, bow to the Speaker, and then take the Oath, or the Affirmation.

An M.P. returned at a by-election is led to the Table by two sponsors, one on each side of him. He may be the only new Member to take the Oath—a terrifying ordeal. As he advances towards the Table, with all eyes upon him, he feels a very solitary figure. After the ceremony, however, the other Members soon make him feel at home. Members from both sides of the House will come up to him in a friendly way and introduce themselves, offering to give him any help he may require in 'settling in'.

The House of Commons is a surprisingly friendly place. In the Chamber, Members on the Government and Opposition

Taking the Oath

benches make violent speeches attacking one another on matters of policy. And yet there is seldom any personal ill feeling between individual Members. After a fierce argument in the House, Members of opposing parties may resort to the Smoking Room or perhaps to one of the bars and chat together on the friendliest terms.

After taking the Oath, a new Member's next ordeal will be his 'maiden speech'. Most new Members feel a natural nervousness when they address the House for the first time. But their apprehension is soon allayed by the courteous reception of their speech—and by the tribute which invariably follows it. It is customary for the next speaker to congratulate the new Member on his maiden speech, and this he will do in glowing terms, regardless of whether in fact he has spoken well or badly. The new Member feels greatly encouraged—until in due time he himself listens to a maiden speech, followed by congratulations couched in similar flowery language.

Gradually he gets the 'feel' of the House, with all its ancient traditions, and most Members settle down to the general routine with complete self-assurance.

When Parliament is sitting an M.P. leads a very busy life. An M.P. who devotes himself entirely to his parliamentary duties may be in the House of Commons (except for occasional short breaks) for at least twelve hours in the day, and sometimes for very much longer. If an important debate is taking place he may on occasion remain in the House until the early hours of the morning, or perhaps all night.

The House sits (*see* Chapter 7) from 2.30 p.m. until 10.30 p.m. every day from Monday to Thursday inclusive, and from 11 a.m. until 4.30 p.m. on Fridays. These are the normal hours of business in the Chamber, but they are sometimes extended for an indefinite period to give extra time for a debate on a major issue.

An M.P. usually spends a certain amount of time in the Chamber each day. He drifts in and out from time to time during the course of the afternoon and evening to listen to any matter that may be of interest to him. He may call in to hear a statement from a minister. He may spend an hour or two listening to a debate on some subject of special concern to his constituency. He may take part in the debate. An M.P. is free to come and go as he pleases, but it is his duty to be in the Chamber to vote for his party if there is a division at the end of a debate. Every Member present in the House of Commons will then pack into the Chamber; whereas at another time—during a dull item of business, of little interest to anyone—there may be no more than perhaps forty or fifty Members scattered about the benches.

A great deal of an M.P.'s time is taken up with committee work. There are three forms of committee with which an M.P. may be concerned: the Standing Committee, the Select Committee and the Party Committee.

The Standing Committees deal with Bills before Parliament (*see* Chapter 7). When a Bill is presented, a Standing Committee is appointed to handle the Bill in its 'committee stage'. The committee is composed of Private Members from both sides of the House—Government and Opposition—the two sides being represented in the same proportions as the House itself is constituted. For example, if a Standing Committee of fifteen were to be appointed and the House comprised about two-thirds Labour Members and one-third Conservative Members, then ten of the Committee would be drawn from the Labour benches and five from the Conservative benches.

After the Bill has received its second reading 'on the floor of the House', it is sent to the Standing Committee for amendment, thereby greatly reducing the amount of work that must be devoted to it in the Chamber—a vital factor if the Government has a heavy programme to complete in a limited period of time. This committee goes through the Bill clause by clause, sentence by sentence, paying the closest attention to every detail, and makes amendments based on the general discussion and on objections raised during the second reading. If the Bill is of a controversial nature this may take several weeks. When the Standing Committee has completed this task the Bill is sent back to the House for consideration of the amendments and for its third and final reading.

A separate Standing Committee is appointed for each Bill, and there may be four or five Bills going through Parliament at the same time. The different committees handling the various Bills are known by the letters of the alphabet—the 'A' Committee, the 'B' Committee, and so on.

The Standing Committees work on the Bills in the mornings,

usually from 10.30 a.m. until 1 p.m., and sometimes also at other times of the day. Members with jobs outside Parliament do very little of this committee work—a sore point with Members who devote all their time to parliamentary business, and who, in consequence, often find themselves overburdened with committee work, for which, incidentally, they receive no extra payment.

The Select Committees deal with such matters as Public Accounts, Public Petitions, Standing Orders, Procedure, Estimates and other subjects which might be referred to them by the House of Commons.

The Party Committees are concerned with matters relating to party policy in the House of Commons.

Each major party has a number of different committees—composed entirely of Private Members—to deal with such matters as housing, transport, education, agriculture, industry and so on. These committees make a regular study of every aspect of their particular subject, and when any matter relating to it is to come before the House they discuss the line of action to be taken by the party.

When Parliament is sitting the Party Committees meet every day between the hours of 4 p.m. and 7 p.m., as a general rule. The meetings are conducted in the strictest secrecy behind closed doors; and, although unfortunately there are occasional 'leaks' to the Press, any Member can feel free to express himself without fear or favour.

Sometimes at these meetings Private Members criticize the actions of ministers. A Party Committee on the Government side—say, the Housing Committee—may be critical of a new plan proposed by the Minister of Housing. If so, the Committee will probably request the Minister to attend a meeting of the Committee—a request which is never refused—so that they can put forward their views to him. The Minister may be able to set their doubts at rest by a more detailed explanation of his plan. On the other hand, if the Private Members are still critical, the Minister may agree to make certain alterations to meet the criticisms. Having gained this concession, the Private Members will support the Minister when his proposals are put before the House.

In this way the Party Committees may—and often do—play an important part in influencing Government policy. Similarly, the Party Committees on the Opposition side may influence the line of action to be taken by their leaders in opposing the Government.

In addition to the individual committees, each party has a general committee—open to all Members—which meets once a week to discuss general policy in the House. The Conservatives have their '1922 Committee', and the Labour Party has a similar committee. At these meetings Members are sometimes strongly critical of their leaders. If they disapprove of a minister's actions, they may press for his resignation. The Prime Minister himself may come in for attack from his party in the House.

An M.P. divides the greater part of his time between committee work and attending sittings in the Chamber. But he also crams a great deal of other work into his day. He may have an appointment with a minister to discuss some problem concerning his constituency. He may have a speech to write. One or two people may call to see him at the House. Anyone is entitled to call at the House of Commons to see his M.P. A visitor is given a 'Green Card' on which he fills in his name and address and states the nature of his business. A messenger then takes the card and goes round the House—to the committee rooms, the library, the Smoking Room, and perhaps the Chamber—and tries to track down the M.P. If the M.P. is available he will see his visitor in the Central Lobby, or possibly in an interview room if he has received prior notice of the visit.

Constituents sometimes call to see their M.P., either singly or

A Member interviewing constituents at the House of Commons

in a small body, to protest against some Government measure, or to endeavour to persuade him to raise some matter in the House—a procedure known as 'lobbying' the M.P., presumably on account of the fact that this usually happens in the Central Lobby.

From time to time an M.P. may also conduct a party round the House—perhaps members of a Women's Institute or Rotary Club, or a party of schoolchildren—and explain the workings of Parliament to them.

And always, every day, he has a heavy mail to deal with. Some people seem to be under the impression that any problem in their lives, great or small, can be solved by their M.P. They may complain to their M.P. if the grass verge in front of their house requires cutting, or if the pavement is not kept clean, or if there are pot-holes in the road, or if there is 'interference' on the television. One man once wrote to his M.P. informing him that his wife had left him three times, and requesting him to take steps to prevent her from doing this a fourth time!

People write to their M.P. about anything and everything. One constant request is for assistance in finding a house—a problem with so many people. It is not however in the province of an M.P. to find houses for people, and he can only pass on such requests to the responsible local authority in his constituency. Indeed this applies to a great many of the requests for assistance made of an M.P.

An M.P. may receive as many as four or five thousand letters in a year. Some are downright stupid. Some are pathetic. Some are extremely sensible and constructive—letters putting forward ideas which the M.P. may decide to take up in the House. He endeavours to answer all letters, the silly as well as the sensible. This is a formidable task. Some M.P.s employ a private secretary to deal with their correspondence; some share a secretary; but the majority make use of the 'pool' of typists in the basement of the House of Commons, since this is the cheapest system. They dictate their letters at odd moments of the day, sandwiching their correspondence between their committee work and their attendance in the Chamber.

An M.P.'s work is not, of course, confined to the House of Commons. He must give time to his constituency too. He must look after the interests of his constituents as a whole, regardless of their party.

Work in the constituency varies greatly according to the nature of the constituency. In an urban or industrial constituency (known as a Borough Constituency) an M.P. will spend a great deal of time examining industrial problems, some of which he may later bring to the notice of a minister. In a rural constituency (known as a County Constituency) an M.P.

will be concerned mainly with agricultural problems. An M.P. in a rural constituency, with perhaps one or two towns and forty or fifty villages to cover, will do a great deal more travelling than an M.P. in an urban constituency. But both will share one thing in common: they will receive constant requests to investigate problems of one kind and another, to address meetings and to attend social functions.

M.P.s do the greater part of their work in the constituencies during the four parliamentary 'recesses', when, for a period of weeks at Easter, Whitsun, summer and Christmas, Parliament is not sitting.

As with most professions, some of an M.P.'s work is very tedious, but in the main it is an exciting life. The greatest excitement is a lively debate in the House, when the Prime Minister and the Leader of the Opposition attack one another 'across the floor', and the House is packed beyond capacity, with all the benches filled and Members overflowing into the gangways and the gallery.

CHAPTER

7

The Commons in Session

THE Chamber of the House of Commons is rectangular in shape, with galleries round the four walls. There is a Distinguished Visitors' Gallery for ambassadors and foreign statesmen; a Peers' Gallery; a Strangers' Gallery for the general public; and a Press Gallery for reporters and correspondents, and a small group of highly paid and highly privileged journalists who not only report the proceedings of Parliament but also inform the public of the background to various political activities. These privileged journalists are known as the 'Press Lobby', and they never break a confidence imparted to them by ministers or Members.

The floor of the Chamber is surprisingly small, being only about 68 feet long and 45 feet wide. It was built to these small dimensions to promote an atmosphere of informality where Members can speak in a conversational style and break in on one another in a way that could never be so effective in a vast hall. Although inadequate for a large attendance of M.P.s at a big debate, the Chamber is an ideal size for an ordinary sitting, when probably no more than two or three hundred Members are likely to be in the Chamber at any one time.

The Chamber is planned in this way. At one end is the

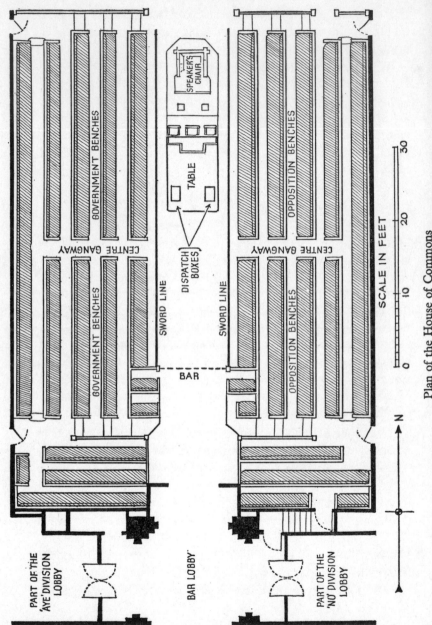

Plan of the House of Commons

imposing raised canopied Chair where the Speaker, dressed in his traditional knee-breeches, long black gown and full-bottomed wig, presides.

Immediately in front of the Speaker is the long Table of the House where Members take the Oath on their election to the Commons. Seated at this Table with their backs to the Speaker are the Clerk of the House and two assistant Clerks, also in wigs and gowns. The Clerk advises the Speaker on questions of order and procedure; and his assistants keep the minutes of the proceedings.

Farther along the Table are two 'Dispatch Boxes'—one on each side—containing copies of the Bible and the Oath. The ministers and leading members of the Opposition stand at the Dispatch Boxes on their respective sides of the Table when addressing the House.

On the far end of the Table rests the Mace, symbol of the Speaker's authority. The Mace lies upon the Table all the time the House is in session, except when it sits as a committee, when it will be placed under the Table.

Five long rows of benches, upholstered in green leather and equipped with sound amplifiers, extend along each side of the Chamber, facing towards each other. The benches on the Speaker's right side are occupied by the Government and its supporters, and those on his left side by the Opposition.

The senior ministers sit on the Front Bench (known as the Treasury Bench) on the Government side. Members of the 'Shadow Cabinet' sit on the Front Bench on the Opposition side. The Shadow Cabinet comprises senior members of the main Opposition party appointed by the Leader of the Opposition to act as spokesmen on different subjects. A 'Shadow Foreign Secretary', for example, will voice the views of the Opposition on foreign affairs and a 'Shadow Chancellor' will speak on financial matters.

The Private Members sit on the benches behind their leaders, and for this reason they are commonly called 'Back-benchers'. They can sit wherever they choose. The benches, however, can accommodate only 437 of the 630 M.P.s, and consequently, at a big debate, many Private Members may have to sit in the galleries.

The Government and Opposition benches are separated by a wide central aisle. This is covered by a carpet with two thick red lines in front of the benches, making a width equivalent to the combined length of two swords, which neither side may cross when speaking—a precaution designed to prevent opposing Members from attacking one another bodily in the heat of a debate!

Beyond the benches, at the end of the Chamber opposite the Speaker, is the Bar of the House—a telescopic brass rod, normally out of sight, which is drawn across the end of the central aisle on special occasions. The Bar marks the official boundary of the Chamber.

The Speaker is the most powerful man in the Commons. An elected Member of Parliament, he is chosen to act as Chairman of the House by the general agreement of M.P.s of all parties. He is elected to the post at the beginning of each Parliament and, once elected, he takes no further part in party politics. He shows strict impartiality to both Government and Opposition. He presides over debates and the general business of the House, controls the proceedings, and sees that the rules are strictly obeyed. His authority over the House is absolute. Even the Prime Minister must bow to his authority and accept his rulings.

The Speaker has two deputies, and is attended by the Serjeant at Arms, who carries the Mace in the Speaker's Procession (*see* page 70); keeps order in the galleries and lobbies; and on rare occasions may be instructed by the Speaker to remove a Member from the Chamber, or perhaps to arrest and bring to the Bar of the House some person who has offended against the dignity of the House.

INTERIOR OF THE HOUSE OF COMMONS

1. Members' side gallery
2. Press gallery
3. Government back benches
4. The Speaker
5. Government front bench
6. Clerks of the House
7. The Mace
8. Dispatch Boxes
9. Opposition front bench
10. Opposition back benches
11. Sword line
12. The Bar of the House

E

The House of Commons must always preserve both its dignity and its authority, and if anyone shows disrespect for its ancient rights and privileges, either by public speech or printed word, the Speaker may request the Committee of Privileges—an all-party committee—to consider whether there has been a 'breach of parliamentary privilege'. If there appears to have been a breach, the Speaker will order the offender to be brought to the Bar (by the Serjeant at Arms) to explain his conduct. Standing before the Bar, he will state his case and apologize with great humility for any offence caused. If the House is not satisfied with his explanation and apology, the offender will be most severely reprimanded, or perhaps even sent to prison. In quite recent times the editor of a daily newspaper was admonished for publishing an article derogatory to the House.

The main functions of the House are to sanction or reject new measures proposed by the Government; to control the actions of departmental ministers by debating their policies and raising questions concerning the conduct of their departments; to grant sums of money, amounting to millions of pounds a year, for Government expenditure; and to assist in making new laws by passing Bills which will eventually become Acts of Parliament. In addition the House will also receive and discuss periodic Petitions from private individuals urging Government action on various matters.

When discussing financial matters (apart from the Budget) the House always sits as a committee—a tradition observed in exercise of the ancient right of the Commons to discuss demands for money privately. When the House goes into committee the Speaker leaves the Chamber, and the Chair is taken by his deputy, the Chairman of Ways and Means, and—since the Speaker is no longer present—the Mace goes under the Table.

The House sits as a committee on many other occasions too. In wartime, or in some national emergency, it may go into committee for secret discussion of some issue which it might not be wise to make public. At such times the Press and all Strangers will be cleared from the galleries.

New Bills, to which a great deal of time is devoted each session of Parliament, are sometimes handled in part by the House sitting as a committee, but more often they are read and discussed with the Speaker in the Chair. Most Bills which come before the House are Government Bills, but a small number are also introduced by Private Members.

The procedure in the case of a Government Bill is as follows. First, the general principles are framed by the Cabinet. The Bill is then worked out in detail by the minister primarily concerned and drafted by a team of Civil Servants, lawyers and experts in various fields. After all these immense preparations have been completed, the Bill is critically examined by the Cabinet, amended if necessary, and finally approved for presentation to Parliament.

The minister concerned then has the task of piloting the Bill through all its stages in the Commons. At the First Reading, the title of the Bill, with no details, is simply read out from a 'dummy' bill. At the Second Reading—by which time copies of the Bill will have been circulated to all Members—the minister presents the Bill in a speech outlining the salient points and stressing the importance of the new measure. The Bill will then be discussed by the House in some detail, and afterwards amendments will be made in the 'committee stage', as described in Chapter 6. The Bill as amended by the Standing Committee is then debated on the floor of the House—the Report Stage—when it may again be amended. Finally the Bill is given its Third Reading.

Sometimes the Government decides to speed the passage of a Bill through the Commons by setting a time-limit for each stage of the discussions—an act, often most unpopular with the Opposition, known as 'imposing the guillotine'.

After passing through the Commons the Bill is given three Readings in the House of Lords. In due time it is returned to the Commons with perhaps further suggestions for amendments, which may or may not be incorporated.

Finally the Bill receives the Royal Assent. The Queen plays no personal part in its enactment. She appoints a Commission comprising the Lord Chancellor and four peers to act for her. The Lords Commissioners sit on the Woolsacks in the House of Lords (*see* Chapter 8); the Commons are summoned to the Lords; and the Royal Assent is given by a Clerk reading out the title of the Bill and a second Clerk then declaring in Norman French: '*La Reine le veult*'—'The Queen desires it.' And so, after months of preparation, discussion and amendment, the Bill becomes an Act of Parliament.

Some Bills are introduced by the Lords, and these of course go through the reverse procedure, passing first through the Lords and then through the Commons.

Most items of business discussed in the Chamber of the Commons take the form of a proposition or motion, made either by a minister or a Private Member, followed by a debate. At the conclusion of the debate the proposition is either carried by assent or else is put to the vote at a division.

The term 'division' is employed because there are two voting lobbies (rooms) leading off the Chamber—an 'Aye' lobby and a 'No' lobby—and Members 'divide' and go into the two different lobbies to vote according to whether they are in favour of or against the motion.

Members on both sides of the House are expected to support their party in every issue that comes up for debate, except in the case of Private Members' Bills and matters on which a 'free vote' is announced. They are expected to follow the 'party line' if they speak in a debate, and to vote at every division except in the instances mentioned.

Each party has a number of 'Whips' to maintain party

Entering a division lobby

discipline. They keep Members regularly informed about everything that is happening, and if there is likely to be a division they instruct them to stand by to vote. There are of course times when it is not possible for a Member to vote: he may be away on parliamentary business, or ill. To guard against this, many Members of opposing parties form 'pairs'. A Member on the Government side will pair with a Member on the Opposition side by standing arrangement. If one of the pair is away or ill, his partner will 'register the pair' at the Whips' Office, and will then refrain from voting himself. Thus each side will lose one vote, and neither party will suffer.

If a Member is strongly opposed to the 'party line' on a particular measure, and feels unable to vote on grounds of conscience, he will inform the Whip, and his feelings will be respected. But if he refrains from voting repeatedly, or 'turns rebel', he may be asked to resign from the party, or possibly he may be expelled—an act known as 'withdrawing the Whip'.

The Leader of the House arranges the general programme of work in the Commons, and the Government Chief Whip, in consultation with him, arranges the day-to-day business. This is an immense and complex task, requiring most careful planning to dovetail everything in. Consideration must be given, not only to the requirements of the Government, but also to the rights of the Opposition and of Private Members to put forward matters for discussion. In each session of Parliament the Opposition are entitled to select items for debate on twenty-eight 'Supply Days' and the Private Members on twenty days. To add to the complications, new issues keep cropping up, and some of the debates, timed to last a certain period, may be extended.

Every Thursday the Leader of the House announces the programme for the following week; and each day an 'Order of the Day' is printed giving the agenda for that day's sitting.

The House normally sits, as previously stated, from 2.30 p.m. until 10.30 p.m. every day from Monday to Thursday, and from 11 a.m. until 4.30 p.m. on Fridays.

The sitting is opened each day by the Speaker's Procession. Preceded by the Serjeant at Arms with the Mace on his right shoulder, the Speaker processes to the Chamber followed by his Train-bearer, Secretary and Chaplain. He crosses the Bar of the House exactly as Big Ben strikes 2.30, or on Fridays 11 o'clock. The Mace is placed on the Table, and the Speaker, after bowing to the assembled Members, walks to the Clerks' end of the Table. He is joined by the Chaplain, who then reads Prayers for two or three minutes. After Prayers the Chaplain retires from the Chamber, bowing. The sitting then begins.

After some formal preliminaries, the first hour will be

devoted to 'Questions'. Every day except Fridays a number of ministers, operating on a roster system, answer questions put to them by Members. A Member wishing to ask a minister a question about his department writes down his question and 'tables' it at the Table Office. All questions addressed to an individual minister must be 'tabled' at least two days before he is due to answer questions.

Each minister on the roster for that day then prepares the answers to the various questions from the different Members in consultation with the senior Civil Servants in his department. The Civil Servants supply him with the necessary information, and may actually write his answers. They also—and most important—try to anticipate and brief the minister for any supplementary questions he may be asked.

All the questions are listed under numbers, and at Question Time Members stand up as their turn comes round and simply cite the relevant number: 'I beg to ask the Minister of Transport Question Number 6.' The minister reads out his prepared answer; and the Member, with the Speaker's consent, may then ask a supplementary question arising out of the answer. If the Civil Servants have not anticipated the 'supplementary', the minister may experience some embarrassment in answering the question.

Indeed, that is the object of some questions—to embarrass ministers. Members on the Opposition side often ask questions designed to bring to light some weakness or inefficiency on the part of the Government. Such tactics are perfectly justifiable, since the possibility of having to answer 'awkward questions' keeps the ministers on their toes, and thereby helps to promote good government. The majority of questions from both sides, however, are designed to seek information; and the ministers may be asked anything up to fifty or a hundred questions.

Sharp at 3.30 Question Time ends. A minister—perhaps the Prime Minister—may then make a statement. Or there may be some small miscellaneous items to be dealt with. Then comes the main business of the day—a debate.

The motion is moved by a minister or a Private Member. The Speaker then 'proposes the question'—summarizes the question to be debated; and the debate proceeds with the Speaker calling upon different Members in turn to speak.

A Member wishing to speak stands up and tries to 'catch the Speaker's eye'. As soon as one Member sits down at the end of his speech, several others will jump to their feet and try to 'catch the Speaker's eye'. Many will spend the whole debate bobbing up and down without being chosen. The Speaker (who can identify every M.P.) glances at those who are standing and calls out a name. If the last speech came from the Government side he will probably select a Member on the Opposition side for the next speech.

The Member selected proceeds to address the House, and the others sit down. He is allowed complete freedom of speech. He cannot be sued for libel or slander in respect of any statements or observations he makes in the House. At the same time he must never use 'unparliamentary language'. If he offends in this, or if he infringes any of the rules of the House, the Speaker will immediately call him to order and demand a withdrawal and apology. If the Member should refuse to withdraw and apologize (which rarely happens) the Speaker may 'name' him—that is, suspend him from the sitting.

If the debate is controversial some Members may have to contend with constant interruptions. An M.P. who wishes to interrupt a speaker to challenge a statement stands up and asks him to 'give way'. The speaker will then either sit down and allow the interrupter to break in, or, if he is not prepared to give way, he will ignore the interruption and continue his speech.

When a number of Members from both sides have spoken, the debate will probably be wound up by a minister.

Among the eleven hundred rooms
in the Palace of Westminster are
interviewing rooms (*above*) in which an M.P.
may see deputations or any other visitors
(see drawing on page 58),
typists' cubicles for the large staff which
deals with Members' correspondence (*right*)
and a room in which reporters
can write their copy and
telephone to their newspapers.

The Clerk of the House of Commons (*left*)
and his two Assistant Clerks.

One of the two
Dispatch Boxes,
containing a copy of
the Bible and of
the Oath taken by
every new M.P.,
on the Table
of the House.

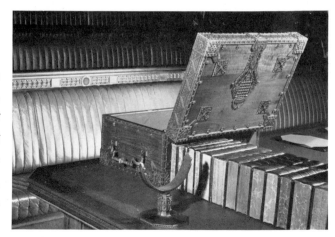

The Cabinet Room at 10 Downing Street.

The Prime Minister sits in the centre of the right-hand side, in front of the portrait of Britain's first Prime Minister, Sir Robert Walpole.

The Bar of the House of Commons,
which is drawn across the central aisle on special occasions.

The light in the tower
above Big Ben shows
that the Commons is sitting
after dark.
When the House adjourns
the light is extinguished.

Members of Parliament take
their seats in the House of Commons.

Entrance to a Division lobby. Members file through the 'Aye' or 'No' lobby according to whether they are voting for or against a motion.
(See drawing on page 69.)

The first step in
a General Election.
The Proclamation by which
the Queen dissolves Parliament.

A candidate
watching his woman agent
briefing a helper.

A candidate hands in
his nomination papers.

A candidate meets
and puts his point of view to
as many people as possible.

Voters arriving at the polling station.
Tellers note down names
or registration numbers.

The Speaker then 'puts the question'. Those in favour of the motion shout 'Aye' and those against it shout 'No'. Unless the response either way is overwhelming, there will probably be a division.

The Speaker orders the lobbies to be cleared. The Division bells are rung, and the call 'Division' echoes through the building. Members hurry from all corners to the voting lobbies. If the debate is on an important issue and the Government has only a very slender majority, the excitement will be tense. Every vote may be vital.

Members stream into the 'Aye' and 'No' lobbies, according to which way they are voting. As they file through their respective lobbies and leave by the exit doors they are counted by Tellers. After six minutes the doors are locked and no more Members may enter the lobbies.

A final count is made of the 'Ayes' and 'Noes', and the Speaker announces the result, showing the majority for or against the motion.

If the Government should be defeated the Opposition will break into shouts of 'Resign! Resign!' The defeat of the Government is, however, normally most unlikely.

At 10 o'clock the main business of the day ends, unless there has been extension of time for the debate. The last half-hour of the sitting is set aside for 'adjournment debates', short discussions usually on constituency problems.

At 10.30 the House adjourns. The Speaker leaves the Chamber, preceded by the Serjeant at Arms. 'Usual time tomorrow,' says the Speaker.

'Home,' calls out the doorkeeper at the Bar of the House. The Division bells are rung, and a light over the top of Big Ben, which shines when the Commons are sitting after dark, is extinguished. Another doorkeeper calls: 'Who goes home?' The cry is taken up by the police in all parts of the building: 'Who goes home? . . . Who goes home?'

8

The House of Lords

THE House of Lords serves two separate functions, one political and the other judicial. In addition to being the Upper House of Parliament, it is also the Supreme Court of Appeal for legal cases in England, Scotland, Wales and Northern Ireland.

There are about nine hundred members of the House of Lords, and they come under two main categories: the Lords Spiritual and the Lords Temporal.

The Lords Spiritual are a very small ecclesiastical body, appointed by ancient right to represent the Church of England. They comprise the Archbishops of Canterbury and York and twenty-four bishops, who are given temporary peerages for the period they are in office. Unlike the Church dignitaries of the past, who wielded great power in Parliament, the Lords Spiritual play no active part in the government of the country. They attend sittings from time to time, and make occasional speeches, but they will never involve the Church in party politics.

The Lords Temporal include hereditary peers—dukes, marquesses, earls, viscounts and barons—whose titles are handed down from father to son; and life peers and peeresses—barons and baronesses—created under the Life Peerage Act of 1958. The hereditary peers of England are supplemented by sixteen Scottish peers, who are elected every Parliament by all the peers of Scotland to represent them in the Upper House.

In addition there are nine judges, known as the Lords of Appeal in Ordinary, who hold life peerages. These Law Lords (as they are commonly called) deal with the judicial business.

The hereditary peers are by far the largest group, numbering approximately eight hundred. Of this number perhaps four hundred come of aristocratic families who have sat in the Lords for two or three centuries or more; two hundred are only the second or third generation of their family to hold the title; and the remaining two hundred or so were themselves raised to the peerage.

Many of the newly created peers were ennobled in reward for their services in various professions. When a Prime Minister retires the Queen may offer him the Order of the Garter and an earldom; and in recent years two Prime Ministers, Earl Attlee and the Earl of Avon (formerly Sir Anthony Eden), accepted peerages and went to the Lords after their retirement. In the Lords today there are a number of former ministers from the Commons who have been raised to the peerage.

Peerages are not given only as a reward for service; they are also created for political reasons. The Prime Minister may decide to send an M.P. to 'Another Place' (as the Commons call the Lords) in order to strengthen his party in the Upper Chamber. Or he may wish to bring some person outside politics—perhaps a financier or an industrialist—into the Government by giving him a seat in the Lords. This can be done simply by requesting the Queen to raise him to the peerage; whereas if the person concerned were to sit in the Commons, a seat would need to be vacated for him, and he would then have to fight a by-election for that seat.

At the beginning of each new Parliament the peers are summoned to the Lords by royal writs. Before taking their seats they take the Oath or the Affirmation and sign the Roll.

75

A great many peers always attend the opening of Parliament to hear the Queen's Speech, but the majority play no part in politics and are seldom, if ever, seen there again.

Of the nine hundred or so peers about a third never set foot in the House of Lords, while another third (commonly known as 'backwoodsmen') attend just occasionally, when some matter of special interest to them comes before the House. Probably no more than 150 peers attend the sittings regularly, and on an average day about a hundred are likely to attend. A peer is paid an expense allowance of four and a half guineas for each day's attendance at the House of Lords.

The set-up in the Lords follows much the same pattern as in the Commons, but differs in points of detail.

At one end of the Chamber, raised on a dais, is the throne, where the Queen sits when opening Parliament.

In front of the throne is the Woolsack—a seat in the form of a large red bench-shaped cushion stuffed with wool—where the Lord Chancellor, head of the Judiciary, presides in legal wig and gown. The Mace, symbol of his authority, rests behind him on the Woolsack when the House is in session, except when it sits as a committee. The Lord Chancellor sits on the Woolsack, according to tradition, because Edward III ordained that the judges should always sit on sacks of wool to remind them of the importance of the wool trade—very great at that time—to the revenue of the country.

Ahead of the Lord Chancellor's Woolsack are two more woolsacks where the judges—the Law Lords—sit at the opening of Parliament.

Immediately in front of them is the Table of the House, at which sit three Clerks: the Clerk of the Parliaments, a Clerk Assistant and a Reading Clerk. A little beyond is a smaller table for the official reporter, who writes a verbatim account of the proceedings.

Ranged along each side of the Chamber—divided by the

76

central aisle occupied by the woolsacks and tables—are five rows of red leather benches, fitted with sound amplifiers. The bishops (the Lords Spiritual) sit on the benches immediately to the right of the Lord Chancellor; and the Government peers sit on the benches beyond the bishops. The benches to the left of the Lord Chancellor are occupied by the Opposition. The peers wear ordinary suits, donning their robes only on special occasions.

There are always many more peers on the Conservative benches than on the Labour benches. There are two main reasons for this. First, the hereditary peers of long lineage are predominantly Conservative, having inherited a Tory tradition from their forbears. Secondly, the Labour Party is a very much younger party, and there has always been a certain reluctance on the part of its members to sit in the Lords on account of the long association of the Upper House with the aristocracy—a reluctance which is gradually breaking down, especially since the introduction of life peers and peeresses from middle-class families.

Some peers do not wish to align themselves with either the Government or the Opposition; they prefer to be independent of party, free to speak and to vote as they wish. These peers sit on cross-benches, which stretch across the Chamber at the end opposite to the throne and Woolsack.

Seated near the cross-benches is the Gentleman Usher of the Black Rod, who carries messages from the Lords to the Commons.

Behind the cross-benches is the Bar of the House, where the Commons, summoned by Black Rod, stand at the opening of Parliament and on other ceremonial occasions when their presence in the Lords may be required. As in the Commons, there are a number of galleries, including a Press Gallery, with a 'Press Lobby' of select and privileged journalists.

The parliamentary work of the Lords is similar to that of the

77

Commons, comprising mainly debates on Government policy and administration, work on new Bills, and a certain amount of committee work. But the volume of business conducted is very much less, and the power of the Lords, once so great, is now very limited. For example, if the Lords object to a Bill sent to them by the Commons, they have no power to reject it. The most they can do is to delay its final enactment by a maximum period of a year. In practice, the Lords very rarely delay a Bill. If they are critical of a Bill they will use their best endeavours to get it improved by suggesting amendments which they hope will prove acceptable to the Commons.

As a general principle, the Lords endeavour to influence Government policy by putting forward suggestions and criticisms of a constructive, rather than destructive, nature. In this way they supplement the work of the Commons and play an important (if lesser) part in the government of the country. Indeed the Commons sometimes pass work on to the Lords to deal with when their own programme is congested.

The judicial business of the Lords is dealt with in the mornings by the Lords of Appeal. The Appeals are heard by a minimum of three Lords of Appeal, and the hearings usually take place in a committee room upstairs. Judgment, either accepting or dismissing an Appeal, is then pronounced in the Chamber, with the Lord Chancellor presiding and the Mace resting on the Woolsack as at a full sitting of the House.

The parliamentary business is conducted in the afternoons. When Parliament is in session the House sits on the afternoons of Tuesday, Wednesday and Thursday, and sometimes also on Monday, each week.

The programme and time-table are arranged by the Leader of the House of Lords, who is the leader of the Government side, and the sitting follows the same general pattern as in the Commons. The sitting is opened by the Lord Chancellor's Procession, followed by Prayers. After formal preliminaries there will be questions to ministers. Very few questions are likely to be asked, however, and—since most of the ministers sit in the Commons—one minister may have to answer for two or three departments besides his own. After Questions there may be a statement by a minister, or some miscellaneous business. Then comes the main item on the agenda—a debate.

There is a striking contrast between a debate in the Lords and a debate in the Commons. Whereas in the Commons the Speaker calls upon Members to speak and controls the debate with rigid discipline and strict impartiality, in the Lords there is no such control.

The Lord Chancellor, presiding, is by no means impartial. A member of the Cabinet, he supports the Government, and he may actually take part in the debate. When he wishes to speak, he leaves the Woolsack and sits on the Government benches as an ordinary peer, returning to the Woolsack after delivering his speech. If there is a division at the end of the debate, he will go into one of the two division lobbies and vote for the Government.

Nobody controls procedure. The peer proposing the motion 'moves for papers'. The Lord Chancellor 'puts the question'— states the question to be debated. The peers then speak without being called upon. They speak in an order previously arranged among themselves. They do not address the Chair as the Commons do. They address the whole House, using the words 'My Lords' as the form of address; and when a peer refers to another peer in a speech he calls him 'the Noble Lord'.

There are very few Standing Orders or rules to be observed. Speakers must adhere strictly to the question before the House. No peer may speak more than once without leave of the House, with the exception of the mover of the motion, who has a right to reply to points raised in the debate. Peers are not expected to read their speeches, although they may speak from notes. And, of course, they must never descend to unparliamentary language.

79

This they never do. The tone is always most courteous. Members who have come from the Lower House, accustomed to the cut-and-thrust of the Commons, sometimes take a little time to adjust themselves to this dignified style of debate. Many find the atmosphere of the Lords rather staid. Nevertheless the standard of debate often reaches a very high level.

At the end of the debate the Lord Chancellor 'collects the voices'. The peers in favour of the motion say 'Content' and those against the motion say 'Not content'. The Lord Chancellor then announces the result. If the result is in doubt there will be a division.

The House of Lords is possibly the only debating chamber in the world where the chairman does not control the proceedings. Yet everything always seems to run smoothly.

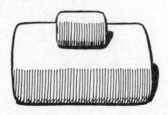

A General Election

THROUGHOUT the life of Parliament the major political parties are preparing all the time, both at party headquarters in London and in the constituencies, for the next General Election, which may come at any moment.

The country is at present divided into 630 parliamentary constituencies. As we have seen, these vary greatly in size and character. A County Constituency may comprise two or three small towns and as many as forty or fifty villages, whereas a Borough Constituency will be confined to a medium-sized town and the surrounding district, or perhaps to a section of a borough or city. In Greater London there are more than forty constituencies.

The boundaries of the constituencies are determined by the Boundary Commissioners, a permanent body set up by agreement of all parties. Each constituency is designed to cover a population of approximately 60,000 people, but a sparsely populated area like the Orkneys has an electorate of only 25,000, and a swiftly growing area like Horsham (Sussex) an electorate of 86,000.

As various areas develop, bringing an increase in population, so the boundaries of the constituencies affected may have to be revised from time to time. This may alter the pattern of voting in a constituency. For example, an influx of industrial workers with Labour sympathies into a predominantly Conservative rural area may turn a 'safe' Conservative seat into a 'marginal' one which, at the next General Election, either party may win.

Each constituency is divided into a number of wards where the local population will vote, and party organization is conducted by each major party through a Constituency Association with branches in the wards.

The branches promote local support for the party, strive to enlist new members, and organize activities such as fêtes, whist drives and so on to raise money to fight the Election whenever it may take place.

The Constituency Association, which is composed of representatives from the branches, supervises party affairs in the constituency as a whole. The Association is headed by an unpaid Chairman with considerable experience of party organization, and working under him is a professional Agent— the king-pin of the Association—who is qualified in election law and party organization. The Chairman and Agent jointly control the 'party machine', and it is they who will conduct the party campaign at a General Election. In a close contest the result may hang largely upon the efficiency of their campaign.

The candidates to contest the seats for the different constituencies are selected in advance of an Election by the party Constituency Associations. The political parties will normally invite all present Members to stand again if they are willing to do so, but it will be necessary for them to find fresh candidates for every new seat they wish to capture. The selectors are likely to be guided in their choice of candidate by his age, personality and general demeanour, among other factors.

In most constituencies the seat will be contested by the two major parties, Conservative and Labour, and in many constituencies the Liberals will also put up a candidate. Each elector is allowed one vote, which he gives to the candidate of his choice.

In a straight fight between two candidates the one elected will receive an actual majority of the votes cast, but this is not always the case in a three-cornered fight. If there are three candidates—Conservative, Labour and Liberal—the one who obtains the most votes will not necessarily have a majority over his two opponents combined. The Conservative and Liberal candidates may together poll more votes than the Labour candidate. Yet, although the majority of the electorate do not vote Labour, the Labour candidate, having won the greatest number of individual votes, will be elected for the division on a 'minority vote'. This is one regrettable weakness in the electoral system.

Every British subject over the age of twenty-one resident in a constituency (with the exception of peers, anyone serving a prison sentence at the time the Register is compiled, and lunatics) is entitled to vote. The right to vote is called the 'suffrage' or 'franchise'. At the present time nearly 36 million people in the British Isles have the franchise, but they can vote only if their names are registered on the Electoral Roll.

In each constituency an Electoral Roll is compiled by the local Registration Officer. Every autumn he sends forms to every house in every street in his district, and the householders are required by law to list the names of all people, including lodgers, resident in their houses at that time, who are over the age of twenty-one or who will be so by a given date. The new Electoral Roll is published the following February; and if a General Election should take place during the next twelve months all whose names appear on the Roll will be allowed to vote in the constituency where they are registered. If a person should be away from home on business at the time he may apply to vote by post, but the 'postal vote' will not be granted to anyone absent from home for private reasons. It will be granted on medical grounds of long-term or permanent incapacity on production of a doctor's certificate. The votes of men and women in the Armed Forces are organized separately.

At every Election a large section of the electorate will always vote Conservative, and another large section will likewise vote Labour. The Liberals also have their firm supporters, in much lesser numbers. It is not, however, the 'die-hard' Conservatives and Socialists who win elections. The result will hinge upon the 'floating voters', who feel no special affinity to any party. They assess the policies, past performances and future promises outlined in the party 'manifestos' (published before an Election) of the different parties, and then vote for the party which, on balance, they consider the best at the time. In many instances they do not make their final decision until the very last moment —perhaps not until polling day. The 'floating voters' hold the key, and as soon as a General Election is announced the major parties will join in battle to capture their votes.

The timing of a General Election rests entirely with the Prime Minister. He studies the trend of public opinion and tries to choose a time most favourable to his party, while also considering the interests of the country and the travelling arrangements of the Queen, who must always be at home during an Election.

The date for the Election having been chosen, the Queen dissolves Parliament, whereupon all Members of Parliament cease to be Members; but, since the government of the country must continue without interruption, the ministers remain in office. After the Dissolution, writs are issued in the Queen's name to the Returning Officers (Mayors or Sheriffs) in the constituencies ordering them to hold a Parliamentary Election in their divisions on the day appointed.

The most stringent rules must be observed by the parties in their election campaigns. They are not allowed to spend more than a stated sum of money. The figure varies according to the constituency: in a County Constituency with an electorate of 60,000 a candidate and his party workers may spend up to £950, and in a Borough Constituency with a similar electorate they may spend £825. These sums must cover all expenses— fees to the Agent, employment of a secretary, printing and stationery, advertising and bill-posting, postage, telephone calls, the hire of rooms for committee purposes and for public meetings, the hire of cars to take supporters to the polling stations, and sundry other expenses. Not a penny more may be spent—and it is an offence for a party supporter to 'help out', as, for example, by lending a room in his house for committee work free of charge. Canvassers, however, are allowed to give their services voluntarily. After the Election the candidate will be required to render an account of the money spent.

There are also rules against corrupt practices, such as bribing, treating, or exerting undue influence on a member of the electorate to gain his vote.

The party Agent is legally responsible for all acts and omissions of the candidate and his supporters. If there should be a breach in election law, a petition may be presented against the successful candidate. The case will be heard by two High Court judges, who will then submit a report to the House of Commons. If corruption is proved, the candidate will be unseated—and the Agent will be liable to a fine, possible imprisonment for a period of up to five years, and disenfranchisement.

The candidates are nominated within eight days of the Dissolution of Parliament. Each candidate is proposed and seconded by members of the electorate, and eight electors sign his nomination paper. He pays a deposit of £150, and this sum will be returned to him after the Election provided that he polls at least one-eighth of the total votes cast; if he fails in this, he will forfeit his deposit.

85

Each candidate normally sends out a printed 'election address', stating his policy, and the G.P.O. deliver this post free to all voters in the constituency. Any information a candidate may require for this will be supplied by his party headquarters, who thereafter will keep him regularly posted with all the latest news and developments in the political scene—data that will assist him in his speeches and canvassing.

Throughout the campaign a party candidate acts on the advice of his Chairman and Agent. He will probably be required to canvass householders for perhaps two hours a day; to travel round the district in a loudspeaker van, addressing people in the streets, for a further hour or so; and to address up to four meetings per evening. He will be expected to meet people in various trades and industries who wish to know his views on policy affecting their own interests; to talk to workers at the factory gates; to visit the market place; to put in an appearance at the railway station in the rush-hour. He will meet and make himself known to as many people as possible.

At the same time, in each ward, teams of voluntary party workers, armed with cards, will go from house to house canvassing people to vote for him, their great aim always being to capture the 'floating voters'. On leaving each house the canvasser marks on the appropriate card the voting intentions (if revealed) of the members of the household. He also enters such details as whether a supporter will require transport to the polling station. All the cards from the different canvassers are subsequently filed in the committee room of the ward for reference on polling day.

Meanwhile the Prime Minister and leading members of the major parties make extensive tours of the 'hustings' to speak in support of their party candidates, paying special attention to the marginal seats, where every vote may count. Many of the leaders also take part in the party political broadcasts on the radio and television. And every day each major party holds a

Press conference to expound and promote its policy—and condemn that of its opponents.

The party leaders have a most exacting time. The Prime Minister is under the double strain of acting as the Queen's first minister, with all its national and international responsibilities, and taking part in the hurly-burly of the hustings.

The period between the Dissolution of Parliament and the actual Election is likely to be anything from three to five weeks. During this period the fortunes of the parties may swing like a pendulum, favouring the Conservatives at one stage and Labour at another stage and then perhaps swinging back to the Conservatives again. So many factors can cause a swing—an unfortunate speech by a minister, a brilliant television performance by a party leader, an international incident, perhaps even a change in the weather.

As the campaign progresses the tempo rises. Excitement mounts as the electorate study the Public Opinion polls in the newspapers. Hecklers multiply and grow noisier. Insults are hurled and parried. . . . To many people with little interest in politics the election period, with all its bickering and backbiting, seems an eternity.

At last polling day arrives. The polling stations in each ward are open from 7 a.m. until 9 p.m. The voting is conducted by secret ballot on forms giving the names of the candidates but not their parties. An elector registers his vote in a 'polling booth'—a small table behind screens. He marks a cross against the name of the candidate of his choice, and then folds his ballot paper and drops it into a sealed ballot box.

In a well-organized constituency the political parties will place Tellers outside each polling station. As the voters leave the polling station after registering their votes the Tellers note down their names or registration numbers on slips of paper. From time to time during the day these slips are taken to the party's committee room, and the names of known supporters

87

who have been to the polls are marked off on a list compiled from the canvassers' cards. In this way a picture is built up. In the latter part of the day 'knockers-up' will go to certain houses and endeavour to rally supporters who have not yet voted. As time begins to run out, the party cars will race hither and thither bringing supporters to the polls.

Sharp at nine o'clock the polling stations close. The ballot boxes are taken from all the polling stations to a central depot— usually the town hall of the principal town in the constituency —and there, under the supervision of the Returning Officer, the thousands of ballot papers are sorted and counted by a team of sorters, running into several hundred, who are sworn to secrecy. First, the number of votes in each box is counted to see that they tally with the number of voters marked off on the list of the polling clerk when they reported at the polling stations. The voting papers are then replaced in the ballot box and subsequently the papers from all the boxes are mixed together and a count is made of the votes for each candidate.

The candidates watch the count and, if the result is very close, the candidate who is narrowly defeated may request the Returning Officer to order a recount. There may be three or four recounts before everyone concerned is satisfied. The speed with which results are announced depends on the number of counters employed by each authority.

The Returning Officer then announces the votes cast for each candidate to the expectant crowds waiting outside, who break into cheers and boos when the name of the elected Member is declared. The successful candidate then makes a short speech, thanking the Returning Officer and his staff for their hard work, and taking the opportunity to thank the electorate for returning him.

The first results usually begin to come through between ten and eleven o'clock. Starting as a trickle, they gradually build up into a steady flow. In homes all over the country people sit up into the early hours of the morning following the results on the radio or television—all anxious to know which party will be returned to power.

If there is a definite swing to either party the result may become obvious during the night, but if the parties are fairly evenly balanced the final result may not be known until the following afternoon. When there can no longer be any doubt about the result the leader of the defeated party will 'concede defeat'. If the party in power is defeated, the Prime Minister will drive to Buckingham Palace and tender his resignation to the Queen, who will then send for the leader of the victorious party and invite him to form a Government.

And so a new Parliament, with either the same or a different party in power, is born.

GLOSSARY

Affirmation. See *Oath.*

Bar of the House. The official boundary of the House of Commons; also of the House of Lords.

Bill. The form in which a proposal for a new law, or amendment to existing law, is put before Parliament.

Black Rod. Officer of the House of Lords, Gentleman Usher to the Lord Chamberlain's department.

Cabinet. Body of Ministers chosen by the Prime Minister to form the chief policy-making instrument of government.

Cap of Maintenance. Cap worn by monarch at the Coronation before being crowned, which is carried in procession at the State opening of Parliament.

Clerk of the House. Officer of the House of Commons responsible for the records of proceedings, etc.

Clerk of the Parliaments. Officer of the House of Lords responsible for the records of proceedings, etc.

Conclusions. Report of the proceedings of a Cabinet meeting.

Dissolution. The end of the life of a parliament, followed by a General Election.

Division. A vote by the Members of Parliament, who 'divide' into the 'Aye' and 'No' lobbies.

Earl Marshal of England. Officer of State, who plays an important part at the State opening of Parliament.

Electoral Roll. Register of persons entitled to vote in an Election, compiled for every constituency.

Floating voters. Voters with no special affinity to a particular political party.

Free vote. In the House of Commons, when Members are not required to vote according to party on certain issues there is said to be a 'free vote'.

Guillotine. The setting of a time limit for discussion of a Bill in the House of Commons.

Leader of the House. Senior minister, appointed by the Prime Minister, responsible for the general programme of parliamentary work.

Lord Great Chamberlain. Officer of State, mainly concerned with ceremonial, and responsible for the buildings of the Palace of Westminster.

91

Lord High Chancellor. Chief Law Lord of England, presides over the House of Lords.

Lord President of the Council. Officer of State who presides over meetings of the Privy Council.

Mace. Symbol of the royal authority vested in the Speaker in the House of Commons and in the Lord Chancellor in the House of Lords.

Oath. Oath of allegiance sworn by new Member of Parliament before the Speaker; those objecting to swearing on oath 'affirm' their allegiance instead. The Oath is sworn by all Members before the opening of every new Parliament.

Order in Council. Document signifying the approval of the Queen on a variety of administrative matters.

Order of the Day. Agenda for a day's sitting of the Commons.

Pairing. Arrangement between political parties whereby if one Member of a 'pair' is unable to vote due to illness, etc., the other, of the opposing party, also refrains.

Party Agent. Paid party constituency worker responsible for conduct of a parliamentary candidate's election campaign, and especially for the amount of money spent.

Party line. The official policy of a political party; Members are expected to vote in the Commons accordingly, except when there is a free vote.

Private Members. Members of Parliament not holding a ministerial post.

Privy Council. Council advising the Queen, from which the modern Cabinet developed.

Proclamation. Document signed by the Queen and bearing the Great Seal of the Realm.

Select Committee. Committee of Private Members dealing with matters referred to them by the House of Commons.

Serjeant at Arms. Officer of the House of Commons, bearer of the Speaker's Mace, and responsible to the Speaker for carrying out instructions for the maintenance of order, etc.

Speaker. Most important officer of the House of Commons, presiding over it impartially.

Standing Committee. Committee of Private Members to consider in detail Bills put before the House.

Whips. Party members appointed to maintain discipline, keep party leaders in touch with trends of opinion among Private Members, etc.

INDEX

94